Qualifications and Credit Framework (QCF)

LEVEL 2 CERTIFICATE IN ACCOUNTING

(QCF)

QUESTION BANK

Basic Accounting I

2012 Edition

First edition 2010
Third edition June 2012

ISBN 9781 4453 9483 1
(Previous ISBN 9780 7517 9756 5)

British Library Cataloguing-in-Publication Data
A catalogue record for this book is available from the British
Library

Published by

BPP Learning Media Ltd
BPP House
Aldine Place
London W12 8AA

www.bpp.com/learningmedia

Printed in the United Kingdom

BPP
LEARNING MEDIA

CONTENTS

Introduction   v

Question and answer bank

Chapter tasks		Questions	Answers
1	Business documentation	3	89
2	Discounts and VAT	5	90
3	The basics of accounting	8	93
4	Accounting for credit sales	13	96
5	Accounting for credit purchases	30	101
6	Double entry bookkeeping	44	106
7	Double entry for sales and trade receivables	52	112
8	Double entry for purchases and trade payables	71	123
9	Initial trial balance	83	132
AAT practice assessment 1		137	157
AAT practice assessment 2		169	191
AAT practice assessment 3		205	227
BPP practice assessment 1: Trappic Ltd		241	263
BPP practice assessment 2: Hazelcombe & Co		275	295
BPP practice assessment 3: Mandarin Ltd		307	329
BPP practice assessment 4: Sumberton Ltd		341	363

BPP
LEARNING MEDIA

INTRODUCTION

This is BPP Learning Media's AAT Question Bank for Basic Accounting I. It is part of a suite of ground breaking resources produced by BPP Learning Media for the AAT's assessments under the qualification and credit framework.

The Basic Accounting I assessment will be **computer assessed**. As well as being available in the traditional paper format, this **Question Bank is available in an online environment** containing tasks similar to those you will encounter in the AAT's testing environment. BPP Learning Media believe that the best way to practise for an online assessment is in an online environment. However, if you are unable to practise in the online environment you will find that all tasks in the paper Question Bank have been written in a style that is as close as possible to the style that you will be presented with in your online assessment.

This Question Bank has been written in conjunction with the BPP Text, and has been carefully designed to enable students to practise all of the learning outcomes and assessment criteria for the units that make up Basic Accounting I. It is fully up to date as at June 2012 and reflects both the AAT's unit guide and the practice assessment(s) provided by the AAT.

This Question Bank contains these key features:

- tasks corresponding to each chapter of the Text. Some tasks are designed for learning purposes, others are of assessment standard
- the AAT's practice assessments and answers for Basic Accounting I and further BPP practice assessments

The emphasis in all tasks and assessments is on the practical application of the skills acquired.

VAT

You may find tasks throughout this Question Bank that need you to calculate or be aware of a rate of VAT. This is stated at 20% in these examples and questions.

Approaching the assessment

When you sit the assessment it is very important that you follow the on screen instructions. This means you need to carefully read the instructions, both on the introduction screens and during specific tasks.

When you access the assessment you should be presented with an introductory screen with information similar to that shown below (taken from the introductory screen from one of the AAT's practice assessments for Basic Accounting I).

This assessment is in TWO sections.
You must show competence in BOTH sections.
You should therefore attempt and aim to complete EVERY task in EACH section.
Each task is independent. You will not need to refer to your answers to previous tasks.
Read every task carefully to make sure you understand what is required.

Where the date is relevant, it is given in the task data.

Both minus signs and brackets can be used to indicate negative numbers UNLESS task instructions say otherwise.

You must use a full stop to indicate a decimal point.
For example, write 100.57 NOT 100,57 or 100 57

You may use a comma to indicate a number in the thousands, but you don't have to.
For example, 10000 and 10,000 are both OK.

Other indicators are not compatible with the computer-marked system.

Section 1   Complete all 6 tasks

Section 2   Complete all 10 tasks

The actual instructions will vary depending on the subject you are studying for. It is very important you read the instructions on the introductory screen and apply them in the assessment. You don't want to lose marks when you know the correct answer just because you have not entered it in the right format.

In general, the rules set out in the AAT practice assessments for the subject you are studying for will apply in the real assessment, but you should again read the information on this screen in the real assessment carefully just to make sure. This screen may also confirm the VAT rate used if applicable.

A full stop is needed to indicate a decimal point. We would recommend using minus signs to indicate negative numbers and leaving out the comma signs to indicate thousands, as this results in a lower number of key strokes and less margin for error when working under time pressure. Having said that, you can use whatever is easiest for you as long as you operate within the rules set out for your particular assessment.

You have to show competence in both sections of assessments and you should therefore complete all of the tasks. Don't leave questions unanswered.

In some assessments written or complex tasks may be human marked. In this case you are given a blank space or table to enter your answer into. You are told in the practice assessments which tasks these are (note: there may be none if all answers are marked by the computer).

If these involve calculations, it is a good idea to decide in advance how you are going to lay out your answers to such tasks by practising answering them on a word document, and certainly you should try all such tasks in this question bank and in the AAT's environment using the practice assessments.

When asked to fill in tables, or gaps, never leave any blank even if you are unsure of the answer. Fill in your best estimate.

Note that for some assessments where there is a lot of scenario information or tables of data provided (e.g. tax tables), you may need to access these via 'pop-ups'. Instructions will be provided on how you can bring up the necessary data during the assessment.

Finally, take note of any task specific instructions once you are in the assessment. For example you may be asked to enter a date in a certain format or to enter a number to a certain number of decimal places.

Remember you can practice the BPP questions in this question bank in an online environment on our dedicated AAT Online page. On the same page is a link to the current AAT practice assessments as well.

If you have any comments about this book, please e-mail paulsutcliffe@bpp.com or write to Paul Sutcliffe, Senior Publishing Manager, BPP Learning Media Ltd, BPP House, Aldine Place, London W12 8AA.

Question bank

Basic Accounting I Question bank

All answers should be rounded to the nearest penny unless otherwise instructed.

Chapter 1

Task 1.1

For each of the following transactions state whether they are cash or credit transactions:

	Cash transaction ✓	Credit transaction ✓
Purchase of goods for £200 payable by cash in one week's time		
Writing a cheque for the purchase of a new computer		
Sale of goods to a customer where the invoice accompanies the goods		
Receipt of a cheque from a customer for goods purchased today		
Purchase of goods where payment is due in three weeks' time		

Task 1.2

When a supplier delivers goods to a customer, the customer will expect to receive in due course:

✓	
	A credit note
	A remittance advice
	A petty cash voucher
	An invoice

Task 1.3

Ken trades in exotic dress materials. He has a large number of small suppliers. He likes to keep all invoices and credit notes from each supplier together in a file for that supplier.

Which sort of coding system would be most appropriate for Ken to use when devising a unique code number for each supplier?

✓	
	An alpha-numeric system
	A numeric system

Chapter 2

Task 2.1

Ken trades in exotic dress materials. He has many credit customers who operate in the same trade as him and he routinely offers these customers a discount off the list price of his goods in order to maintain good relations. This is an example of:

✓	
	A trade discount
	A settlement discount
	A bulk discount
	A discount for prompt payment

Task 2.2

VAT is a tax on consumer expenditure which a VAT registered business must collect from its customers and pay over to

✓	
	The Home Office
	The Treasury
	The Inland Revenue
	HM Revenue and Customs

Task 2.3

On your desk is a pile of sales invoices that have already had the price of the goods entered onto them and been totalled.

You now have to calculate and deduct the 15% trade discount that is allowed on each of these invoices.

Goods total	Trade discount £	Net total £
£416.80		
£105.60		
£96.40		
£263.20		
£351.00		

Task 2.4

There is a further pile of invoices which have the net total entered for which you are required to calculate the VAT charge and the invoice total.

Net total	VAT £	Invoice total £
£258.90		
£316.80		
£82.60		
£152.70		
£451.30		

Task 2.5

You now discover that for each of the invoices from the previous activity a 3% settlement discount has been offered.

Recalculate the VAT charge to correctly reflect the settlement discount and show the revised invoice total (remember that VAT is always rounded down to the nearest penny).

Net total	VAT £	Invoice total £
£258.90		
£316.80		
£82.60		
£152.70		
£451.30		

Task 2.6

The following invoice totals include VAT (no settlement discount is available).

Calculate the amount of VAT on each invoice and the net amount of the invoice:

Invoice total £	VAT £	Net total £
145.20		
66.90		
246.60		
35.40		
125.40		

Task 2.7

The following purchases have been made for cash inclusive of VAT.

Calculate the amount of VAT on each purchase and the net amount of the purchase:

Invoice total £	VAT £	Net total £
252.66		
169.20		
48.60		
104.28		
60.48		
822.60		

Chapter 3

Task 3.1

Ken trades in exotic dress materials. He sends an invoice for goods of £100 plus VAT to a customer. No discounts apply. The invoice total will be:

£ [   ]

Task 3.2

Ken sends an invoice for goods of £100 plus VAT to a customer to whom he allows a 10% trade discount. The invoice total will be:

£ [   ]

Task 3.3

Natural Productions is a small business that manufactures a variety of soaps and bath products which it sells directly to shops. During January 20XX the following credit sales to customers took place:

Invoice No. 6237 to Hoppers Ltd £547 plus VAT
Invoice No. 6238 to Body Perfect £620 plus VAT
Invoice No. 6239 to Esporta Leisure £346 plus VAT
Invoice No. 6240 to Langans Beauty £228 plus VAT
Invoice No. 6241 to Body Perfect £548 plus VAT
Invoice No. 6242 to Superior Products £221 plus VAT
Invoice No. 6243 to Esporta Leisure £416 plus VAT
Invoice No. 6244 to Hoppers Ltd £238 plus VAT
Invoice No. 6245 to Langans Beauty £274 plus VAT

You are required to:

(a) **Enter these transactions into the sales day book given below**

(b) **Cast the columns of the sales day book and check that they cross cast**

Sales day book

Customer	Invoice number	Invoice total £	VAT £	Net £

Cross-cast check:

	£
Net	
VAT	—
Invoice total	＝

Task 3.4

During January the following credit notes were issued by Natural Productions to various customers:

Credit note No. 1476 to Hoppers Ltd £68.70 plus VAT

Credit note No. 1477 to Esporta Leisure £89.20 plus VAT

Credit note No. 1478 to Superior Products £11.75 plus VAT

You are required to:

(a) **Enter these transactions into the sales returns day book given below**

(b) **Cast the columns of the sales returns day book and check that they cross cast**

Sales returns day book

Customer	Credit note number	Credit note total £	VAT £	Net £

Cross-cast check:

	£
Net	
VAT	—
Credit note total	=

Task 3.5

Natural Productions manufactures a variety of soaps and bath products. It buys materials for the manufacturing process from a number of suppliers on credit. It also buys other items such as stationery and packaging on credit. During January 20XX Natural Productions received the following invoices from credit suppliers:

4 Jan   Invoice No. 03576 from P J Phillips £357 plus VAT for materials
6 Jan   Invoice No. 18435 from Trenter Ltd £428 plus VAT for materials
9 Jan   Invoice No. 43654 from W J Jones £210 plus VAT for stationery
12 Jan Invoice No. 03598 from P J Phillips £413 plus VAT for materials
16 Jan Invoice No. 28423 from Packing Supplies £268 plus VAT for packaging
19 Jan Invoice No. 18478 from Trenter Ltd £521 plus VAT for materials
20 Jan Invoice No. 84335 from O & P Ltd £624 plus VAT for materials
24 Jan Invoice No. 28444 from Packing Supplies £164 plus VAT for packaging
28 Jan Invoice No. 18491 from Trenter Ltd £368 plus VAT for materials
31 Jan Invoice No. 43681 from W J Jones £104 plus VAT for stationery

You are required to:

(a) **Enter these transactions in the purchases day book given below**

(b) **Cast the columns of the purchases day book and check that they cross cast**

Purchases day book

Date	Supplier	Invoice number	Invoice total £	VAT £	Purchases (materials) £	Stationery £	Packaging £

Cross-cast check:

	£
Packaging	
Stationery	
Purchases (materials)	
VAT	
Invoice total	

Task 3.6

During January Natural Productions received the following credit notes from suppliers in relation to the invoices set out in Task 3.3:

10 Jan Credit note No. 04216 from P J Phillips materials of £98 plus VAT
16 Jan Credit note No. CN 0643 from W J Jones stationery of £56 plus VAT
30 Jan Credit note No. CN 1102 from O & P Ltd materials of £124 plus VAT

You are required to:

(a) **Enter these transactions in the purchases returns day book given below**

(b) **Cast the columns of the purchases returns day book and check that they cross cast**

Purchases returns day book

Date	Supplier	Credit note number	Credit note total £	VAT £	Purchases (materials) £	Stationery £	Packaging £

Cross-cast check:

	£
Packaging	
Stationery	
Purchases (materials)	
VAT	‾‾‾‾‾
Credit note total	‾‾‾‾‾

Chapter 4

Task 4.1

Ken trades in exotic dress materials. A new customer has phoned up with an enquiry about buying some materials from Ken.

What should Ken send the customer?

✓	
	A delivery note
	A price list
	A goods received note
	A statement of account

Task 4.2

Ken wishes to analyse his sales so that he can distinguish between those made to UK customers and those from abroad.

What is the best way for him to do this?

✓	
	Analyse every invoice into a separate column of his analysed sales day book
	Allocate one of two sales codes to each invoice and use this to write up the invoices in the analysed sales day book
	Allocate invoice numbers on a randomised basis
	Use a different sequence of invoice numbers for each customer

Task 4.3

You work in the accounts department for Southfield Electrical and on your desk are three purchase orders received from customers today. The purchase orders have already been checked to the purchase quotations and the list prices are correct on each purchase order.

You also have on your desk the customer details file which gives you the following information about the three customers:

Customer name	Customer code	Trade discount	Settlement discount
Whitehill Superstores	SL 44	10%	4% – 10 days
Quinn Ltd	SL 04	15%	–
Harper & Sons	SL 26	10%	3% – 14 days

You are required to complete the three blank sales invoices given for each of these purchase orders.

The last sales invoice sent out was 57103. Today's date is 8 January 20XX. If no settlement discount is offered or taken then payment is due within 30 days.

PURCHASE ORDER

WHITEHILL SUPERSTORES
28 Whitehill Park
Benham DR6 5LM
Tel 0303446 Fax 0303447

To: Southfield Electrical
Industrial Estate
Benham DR6 2FF

Number: 32431

Date: 4 Jan 20XX

Delivery address: Whitehill Superstores
28, Whitehill Park
Benham DR6 5LM

Product code	Quantity	Description	Unit list price £
6060	8	Hosch Tumble Dryer	300.00

Authorised by: *P. Williams* **Date:** *04/01/XX*

PURCHASE ORDER

QUINN LTD
High Rocks Estate
Drenchley
DR22 6PQ
Tel 0310442 Fax 0310443

To: Southfield Electrical
    Industrial Estate
    Benham DR6 2FF

Number: 24316

Date: 5 Jan 20XX

Delivery address: As above

Product code	Quantity	Description	Unit list price £
3170	14	Temax Mixer	35.00

Authorised by: *J. P. Walters*

Date: *05/01/XX*

PURCHASE ORDER

HARPER & SONS
30/34 High Street
Benham DR6 4ST
Tel 0303419 Fax 0303464

To: Southfield Electrical
Industrial Estate
Benham DR6 2FF

Number: 04367

Date: 4 Jan 20XX

Delivery address: 30/34 High Street
Benham DR6 4ST

Product code	Quantity	Description	Unit list price £
6150	3	Hosch Washing Machine	260.00

Authorised by: _S. Stevens_   **Date:** 5 Jan 20XX

INVOICE number			
Southfield Electrical, Industrial Estate, Benham DR6 2FF			
VAT registration:	0264 2274 49		
Date/tax point:			
Order number:			
Customer:	Whitehill Superstores		
Account number (customer code)			
Product code	Quantity	Unit amount £	Total £
Trade discount		%	
Net total			
VAT at 20%			
Invoice total			
Settlement discount			%

INVOICE number			
Southfield Electrical, Industrial Estate, Benham DR6 2FF			
VAT registration:	0264 2274 49		
Date/tax point:			
Order number:			
Customer name:	Quinn Ltd		
Account number (customer code)			
Product code	Quantity	Unit amount £	Total £
Trade discount	%		
Net total			
VAT at 20%			
Invoice total			
Settlement discount			%

INVOICE number			
Southfield Electrical, Industrial Estate, Benham DR6 2FF			
VAT registration:	0264 2274 49		
Date/tax point:			
Order number:			
Customer:	Harper & Sons		
Account number (customer code)			
Product code	Quantity	Unit amount £	Total £
Trade discount	%		
Net total			
VAT at 20%			
Invoice total			
Settlement discount			%

Task 4.4

You work in the accounts department of Whitehill Superstores. Given below are a purchase order and related delivery note and sales invoice in respect of a purchase of goods from Southfield Electrical.

You are required to check the documents carefully and note any problems that you discover, stating how you would deal with them.

PURCHASE ORDER

WHITEHILL SUPERSTORES
28 Whitehill Park
Benham DR6 5LM
Tel 0303446 Fax 0303447

To: Southfield Electrical
Industrial Estate
Benham
DR6 2FF

Number: 32202

Date: 16 Oct 20XX

Delivery address: Whitehill Superstores
28, Whitehill Park
Benham DR6 5LM

Product code	Quantity	Description	Unit list price £
7460	11	Magifen Vacuum	210.00
3264	7	Temax Food Processor	65.00
9406	15	Kensharp Toaster	15.00

Authorised by: *P. Winterbottom*　　　　**Date:** 16 Oct 20XX

DELIVERY NOTE

Southfield Electrical
Industrial Estate
Benham DR6 2FF
Tel 0303379 Fax 0303152

Delivery address:

Whitehill Superstores
28, Whitehill Park
Benham DR6 5LM

Number: 34816
Date: 18 Oct 20XX
Order number: 32202

Product code	Quantity	Description
3264	7	Temax Food Processor
9406	12	Kensharp Toaster
7460	11	Magifen Vacuum

Received by: [Signature] *J. Jones*   **Print name:** J. Jones

Date: 18 Oct 20XX

INVOICE

Southfield Electrical
Industrial Estate
Benham DR6 2FF
Tel 0303379 Fax 0303152
VAT Reg 0264 2274 49

To: Whitehill Superstores
28, Whitehill Park
Benham DR6 5LM

Invoice number: 56501

Date/tax point: 22 Oct 20XX

Order number: 32202

Account number: SL 44

Quantity	Description	Stock code	Unit amount £	Total £
7	Temax Food Processor	3264	65.00	455.00
15	Kensharp Toaster	9406	15.00	225.00
11	Magifen Vacuum	7460	220.00	2,420.00
				3,100.00
Less:	10% discount			310.00

Net total	2,790.00
VAT	535.68
Invoice total	3,325.68

Terms
4% discount for settlement within 10 days of invoice date, otherwise net 30 days
E & OE
Carriage Paid

Task 4.5

Given below is a credit note for a customer which receives 20% trade discount.

You are required to check it carefully, state what is wrong with it and calculate the correct figures. Remember that VAT must be rounded down to the nearest penny, though other figures may be rounded up to the nearest penny if appropriate.

CREDIT NOTE

SOUTHFIELD ELECTRICAL
INDUSTRIAL ESTATE
Benham DR6 2FF
Tel 0303379 Fax 0303152
VAT Reg 0264 2274 49

To:

B. B. Berry Ltd
Industrial Estate
Benham
DR6 5FW

Credit note number: 08669

Date/tax point: 22 Oct 20XX

Order number 40102

Account number: 5416

Quantity	Description	Stock code	Unit amount	Total
			£	£
3	Zanpoint fridge	4770	220.00	660.00
2	Temax whisk	3212	6.99	19.38
			Net total	679.38
			VAT	135.88
			Gross total	543.50

Reason for credit note:

Goods not ordered

Task 4.6

You work in the accounts department of Southfield Electrical. You have been given the two credit notes below. You are told that settlement discount is not relevant to the calculations on them.

You are required to:

(a) **Use the credit notes to write up the sales returns day book, and**

(b) **Total the sales returns day book**

Sales returns day book

Date	Customer	Credit note number	Customer code	Credit note total £	VAT £	Net £
	Totals					

CREDIT NOTE

SOUTHFIELD ELECTRICAL
INDUSTRIAL ESTATE
Benham DR6 2FF
Tel 0303379 Fax 0303152
VAT Reg 0264 2274 49

Invoice to:

Whitehill Superstores
28 Whitehill Park
Benham DR6 5LM

Credit note number: 08650
Date/tax point: 21 Sept 20XX
Order number 6021
Account number: SL 44

Quantity	Description	Stock code	Unit amount £	Total £
1	Zanpoint Fridge	3676	330.00	330.00
Less:	10% discount			33.00

Net total	297.00
VAT	59.40
Gross total	356.40

Reason for credit note:

Damaged goods

CREDIT NOTE

SOUTHFIELD ELECTRICAL
INDUSTRIAL ESTATE
Benham DR6 2FF
Tel 0303379 Fax 0303152
VAT Reg 0264 2274 49

Invoice to:

Dagwell Enterprises
Dagwell House
Hopchurch Rd
Winnish
DR2 6LT

Credit note number: 08651
Date/tax point: 23 Sept 20XX
Order number 5983
Account number: SL 15

Quantity	Description	Stock code	Unit amount	Total
			£	£
6	Temax Coffee maker	6470	40.00	240.00
Less:	15% discount			36.00
			Net total	204.00
			VAT	40.80
			Gross total	244.80

Reason for credit note:

Goods not ordered

Task 4.7

You work in the accounts department of Southfield Electrical. The following are extracts from the day books relating to transactions in May 20XX with Alpha Services & Co. together with a remittance advice note for a cheque payment received in May 20XX from the customer.

You are required to enter the transactions in the sales ledger and prepare a statement of account for Alpha Services as at the end of May 20XX.

Sales day book – extract

Date 20XX	Customer	Invoice number	Customer code	Total £	VAT £	Net £
7 May	Alpha Services	715	SL10	5,190.00	865.00	4,325.00
17 May	Alpha Services	787	SL10	10,020.00	1,670.00	8,350.00

Sales returns day book – extract

Date 20XX	Customer	Credit note number	Customer code	Total £	VAT £	Net £
12 May	Alpha Services	551	SL10	624.00	104.00	520.00

REMITTANCE ADVICE NOTE	Remittance advice note number 013278
Alpha Services 83 Abbey Road Durringham DU5 2WP	
Supplier:	Southfield Electrical Industrial Estate Benham DR6 2FF
Account number (supplier code)	PL 821

Date	Transaction reference	Amount £
21/04/XX	Invoice 600	289.50
27/04/XX	Credit note 401	(35.87)
1/5/XX	Payment made – cheque enclosed	253.63

Sales ledger

Alpha Services

SL 10

Details	£	Details	£
Balance b/d	253.63		

STATEMENT OF ACCOUNT

Southfield Electrical

Industrial Estate

Benham DR6 2FF

Tel: 01239 345639

VAT registration:	0264 2274 49
Date:	
Customer:	Alpha Services 83 Abbey Road Durringham DU5 2WP
Account number (customer code)	

Date	Details	Debit £	Credit £	Balance £
Amount now due				

Task 4.8

Given below are two cheques received by Southfield Electrical, today 20 November 20XX, together with extracts from the sales invoices that are being paid in each case.

Check that the correct amount has been paid and if not explain where the error has been made.

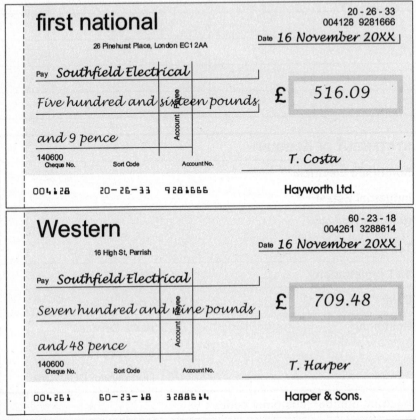

Invoice number	30227	
Date:	7 November 20XX	
To:	Hayworth Ltd	
		£
Goods value		448.00
VAT		86.01
Invoice total		534.01

4% settlement discount for payment received within 10 days of invoice date, otherwise 30 days net

Invoice number	**30256**	
Date:	12 November XX	
To:	Harper & Sons	
		£
Goods value		620.00
VAT		119.04
Invoice total		739.04

4% settlement discount for payment received within 10 days of invoice date, otherwise 30 days net

Chapter 5

Task 5.1

Ken trades in exotic dress materials.

Complete the following sentence:

When a supplier delivers materials to him he retains the supplier's delivery note and also prepares a [   ] once he has had a chance to inspect the quality of the items.

Task 5.2

Complete the following sentence:

A code which will help Ken to classify the different types of material purchase when completing his analysed purchases day book is

✓	
	A supplier code
	A product code

Task 5.3

Ken has been offered a settlement discount by one of his suppliers of '2% for payment within 10 days'. He receives an invoice date 10 June on 12 June with an invoice total of £239.20, which includes VAT of £39.20. He wishes to take advantage of the discount.

By what date must the supplier receive the payment?

[   ]

How much should Ken pay the supplier on that date?

£ [   ]

Task 5.4

You work for Newmans, a music shop, in the accounts department and one of your responsibilities is to organise the payments to suppliers. You have been off sick for the last

week and a half and therefore it is urgent that you consider the invoices that are on your desk requiring payment.

Newmans' policy is to pay any invoices that are due each Friday. When a cheque is written on a Friday it does not then reach the supplier until Monday, ie three days later. If a settlement discount is offered by a supplier then this is taken if the discount will still be valid on the Monday. Otherwise the policy is to take the maximum amount of credit available.

Today's date is Friday 27 January 20XX. Thereafter, the following payment dates are 3 February, 10 February and 17 February. Remember that, as payments take three days to reach the supplier, any invoice dated earlier than 7 January with a 30-day period must be paid today, because if they are delayed until 3 February then the payments will not be received until 6 February, more than 30 days after they are due.

The invoices that are on your desk are scheduled below:

Invoice date	Supplier name	Terms	Total £	VAT £	Net £
5 Jan	Henson Press	30 days	336.00	56.00	280.00
8 Jan	GH Publications	30 days	136.80	22.80	114.00
12 Jan	Ely Instruments	20 days 2% discount otherwise 30 days	765.44	125.44	640.00
15 Jan	Hams Instruments	14 days 2.5% discount otherwise 30 days	370.45	60.45	310.00
19 Jan	CD Supplies	10 days 3% discount otherwise 30 days	138.02	22.42	115.60
22 Jan	Jester Press	10 days 3.5% discount otherwise 30 days	152.22	24.62	127.60
22 Jan	Henson Press	30 days	306.00	51.00	255.00
23 Jan	CD Supplies	10 days 3% discount otherwise 30 days	78.08	12.68	65.40
25 Jan	Jester Press	10 days 3.5% discount otherwise 30 days	47.12	7.62	39.50
25 Jan	Buser Ltd	7 days 5% discount otherwise 30 days	291.55	46.55	245.00

In the schedule given below show the date that each invoice should be paid and the amount for which the cheque should be written out.

Invoice date	Supplier name	Payment date	Working	Amount of cheque £
5 Jan	Henson Press			
8 Jan	GH Publications			
12 Jan	Ely Instruments			
15 Jan	Hams Instruments			
19 Jan	CD Supplies			
22 Jan	Jester Press			
22 Jan	Henson Press			
23 Jan	CD Supplies			
25 Jan	Jester Press			
25 Jan	Buser Ltd			

Task 5.5

Given below is a statement received by your organisation, Edgehill Designs, from one of its credit suppliers, P T Supplies, as at 31 January 20XX. You are instructed to pay all of the invoices less credit notes up to 10 January. Today's date is 7 February.

You are required to complete the remittance advice attached to the statement. Note that this supplier does not offer a settlement discount to your organisation.

STATEMENT

P. T. Supplies
28 Farm Court Road
Drenchley DR22 4XT

To: Edgehill Designs

Account number: SL 53

Date: 31 January 20XX

Date	Details	Debit	Credit	Balance
1 Jan	Balance b/f	227.63		227.63
6 Jan	Inv 20671	107.22		334.85
8 Jan	Inv 20692	157.63		492.48
9 Jan	Payment - Thank you		227.63	264.85
10 Jan	CN 04722		28.41	236.44
17 Jan	Inv 20718	120.48		356.92
25 Jan	Inv 20734	106.18		463.10
30 Jan	CN 04786		16.15	446.95

Amount now due | £446.95

REMITTANCE ADVICE

To: P.T. Supplies
28 Farm Court Road
Drenchley Dr22 4XT

From: Edgehill Designs

Date:

Reference	Amount £	Paid ✓

CHEQUE ENCLOSED

Task 5.6

Given below is an invoice received by Whitehill Superstores. You are also given the related purchase order, delivery note and GRN.

You are required to check the invoice thoroughly and note any problems that you discover.

GOODS RECEIVED NOTE

	GRN number:	47422
Supplier: Southfield Electrical	**Date:**	16 Sept 20XX
	Order number:	32103
	Delivery Note No:	34660

Quantity	Description	Stock code
10	A3 Night Light	9116
6	Zanpoint Tumble Dryer	4560

Received by: L Daniels

Checked by: D Richards

Comments: All in good condition

DELIVERY NOTE

Southfield Electrical
Industrial Estate
Benham DR6 2FF
Tel 0303379 Fax 0303152

Delivery address:

Whitehill Superstores
28, Whitehill Park
Benham DR6 5LM

Number: 34660
Date: 15 Sept 20XX
Order number: 32103

Product code	Quantity	Description
9116	10	A3 Night Light
4560	6	Zanpoint Tumble Dryer

Received by: [Signature] *L Daniels*   **Print name:** L Daniels

Date: 15 Sept 20XX

PURCHASE ORDER

WHITEHILL SUPERSTORES
28 Whitehill Park
Benham DR6 5LM
Tel 0303446 Fax 0303447

To: Southfield Electrical
Industrial Estate
Benham
DR6 2FF

Number: 32103
Date: 10 Sept 20XX

Delivery address: As above

Product code	Quantity	Description	Price
4560	7	Zanpoint Tumble Dryer	245.00
9116	10	A3 Night light	24.58

Authorised by: *P. Winterbottom*   **Date:** 10 Sept 20XX

INVOICE

Southfield Electrical
Industrial Estate
Benham DR6 2FF
Tel 0303379 Fax 0303152
VAT Reg 0264 2274 49

To: Whitehill Superstores
28, Whitehill Park
Benham DR6 5LM

Invoice number: 56389

Date/tax point: 2 Oct 20XX

Order number: 32103

Account number: SL 44

Quantity	Description	Stock code	Unit amount £	Total £
7	Zanpoint Tumble Dryer	4560	245.00	1,778.00
10	A3 Night lights	9116	24.58	245.80
				2023.80
Less:	10% discount			202.38

Net total	1,821.42
VAT	364.28
Invoice total	2,185.70

Terms
4% discount for settlement within 10 days, otherwise 30 days net
E & OE
Carriage paid

Task 5.7

Given below is an invoice received by Dartmouth Supplies and the related purchase order and delivery note. The supplier's file shows that a 10% trade discount is normally given but no settlement discount is offered.

You are required to check this invoice thoroughly and to note any problems that you discover.

INVOICE

Dan Industrials
Park Rise
Fenbridge DR2 7AD
Tel 0461222 Fax 461223
VAT Reg 0621 3384 20

To: Dartmouth Supplies
Fenbridge Estate North
Fenbridge
DR2 6PQ

Invoice number: 77412

Date/tax point: 7 Oct 20XX

Order number: 317428

Account number: SL 116

Quantity	Description	Stock code	Unit amount £	Total £
24	Regent Chair	C11	40.50	972.00
16	Imperial Desk	D46	96.00	1,536.00

Net total	2,535.00
VAT	507.00
Invoice total	3,042.00

Terms
Net 30 days
E & OE

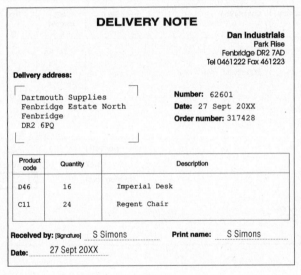

Task 5.8

You have been given an extract from your organisation's purchases day book in respect of credit transactions taking place in June. No entries have yet been made in the ledgers.

Information from the suppliers' files indicate that Seashell Ltd offers a 10% settlement discount for payment within 10 days. Opal & Co does not offer a settlement discount. Both suppliers charge VAT on sales.

You are required to complete the purchases day book and state what the entries will be in the purchases ledger.

Purchases day book

Date 20XX	Details	Invoice number	Total £	VAT £	Net £
30 June	Seashell Ltd	8971			3,211.00
30 June	Opal & Co	05119	4,800.00		
	Totals				

Purchases ledger

Account name	Amount £	Debit ✓	Credit ✓
▼			
▼			

Picklist:

Seashell Ltd
Opal & Co
Net
Purchases
Purchases ledger control
Purchases returns
Sales
Sales ledger control
Sales returns
Total
VAT

Task 5.9

You work for Bailie Ltd. Shown below is a statement of account received from a credit supplier, Dazzle Ltd, and the supplier's account as shown in the purchases ledger of Bailie Ltd.

Dazzle Ltd
21 Albert Street
Keeley
KE4 7AB

To: Bailie Ltd
5 Purley Road
Keeley
KE5 7LW

STATEMENT OF ACCOUNT

Date 20XX	Reference	Details	Debit £	Credit £	Balance £
1 July	8371	Goods	335		335
3 July	8412	Goods	420		755
7 July	8515	Goods	723		1,478
10 July	CN 3215	Goods returned		250	1,228
16 July		Cheque		485	743

Purchases ledger – Dazzle Ltd

Date 20XX	Details	Amount £	Date 20XX	Details	Amount £
15 July	Bank – cheque	485	1 July	PDB 8371	335
15 July	Discount received	20	3 July	PDB 8412	420
			7 July	PDB 8515	723

(a) **Which item is missing from the statement of account from Dazzle Ltd?**

(b) **Which item is missing from the supplier account in Bailie Ltd's purchases ledger?**

(c) **Assuming any differences between the statement of account from Dazzle Ltd and the supplier account in Bailie Ltd's purchases ledger are simply due to omission errors, what is the amount owing to Dazzle Ltd?**

£ [   ]

Task 5.10

A supply of nails has been delivered to Acute Carpentry by Carbon Irons. The purchase order sent from Acute Carpentry, and the invoice from Carbon Irons, are shown below.

Acute Carpentry

Purchase Order No. 78639

To: Carbon Irons

Date: 16 June

Please supply 30 boxes 6" nails product code N1106
Purchase price: £20 per box, plus VAT
Discount: less 10% trade discount, as agreed.

Carbon Irons
Invoice No. 2318

Acute Carpentry

18 June

30 .... boxes product code N1106 @ £25 each	£750.00
VAT @ 20%	£150.00
Total	£900.00

Terms: 30 days net

Check the invoice against the purchase order and answer the following questions.

	Yes ✓	No ✓
Has the correct purchase price of the cardboard boxes been charged?		
Has the correct discount been applied?		
What would be the VAT amount charged if the invoice was correct?	£	
What would be the total amount charged if the invoice was correct?	£	

Task 5.11

Ken runs a business trading in exotic dress materials. He sends out cheques to suppliers on the last day of the month following the month of invoice. Below is an extract from Ken's purchases ledger for his supplier, Mack Materials.

Mack Materials

Date 20XX	Details	Amount £	Date 20XX	Details	Amount £
31 May	Bank	890	1 May	Balance b/d	890
19 May	Purchases returns credit note 43	31	7 May	Purchases Invoice 901	760
			3 June	Purchases Invoice 963	189

(a) **Complete the remittance advice note below.**

Ken's Exotics
1 Bath Street
Cembury, CE11 9SD

REMITTANCE ADVICE

To: Mack Materials   Date: 30 June 20XX

Please find attached our cheque in payment of the following amounts.

Invoice number	Credit note number	Amount £
Total amount paid		

(b) **Which of the following statements is true?**

	✓
The remittance advice note will be sent to the accounts department at Mack Materials to request that a cheque is raised	
The remittance advice note will be sent to Mack Materials' bank to advise them of the amount being paid	
The remittance advice note will be sent to the customer to advise them of the amount being paid	
The remittance advice note will be sent to the supplier to advise them of the amount being paid	

Task 5.12

Ken has received a statement from a supplier which shows that, as at the end of June 20XX, he owes the supplier £2,876. The purchases ledger account for this supplier shows that at that date Ken only owed £1,290.

Which of the following items would explain the difference?

	✓
Ken has requested a credit note from the supplier for £1,586 which he has not yet received	
Ken sent a cheque for £1,586 to the supplier on 30 June 20XX	
Ken ordered some items from the supplier on 30 June for £1,586 but the goods have not yet been delivered and an invoice has not yet been raised	

Chapter 6

Task 6.1

Identify whether each of the following is an asset or a liability:

	Asset ✓	Liability ✓
A trade receivable		
A car used in the business		
A loan from the bank		
A bank overdraft		
Cash in hand		
VAT owed to HMRC		
A trade payable		

Task 6.2

Complete the following sentences using the word 'debit' or 'credit' in each case:

An increase in an expense is a [   ]

A decrease in a liability is a [   ]

An increase in income is a [   ]

An increase in an asset is a [   ]

An increase in capital is a [   ]

A decrease in an asset is a [   ]

An increase in a liability is a [   ]

A decrease in capital is a [   ]

Task 6.3

State the two effects of each of these transactions in the space given below.

(i)   James paid £20,000 into a business bank account in order to start the business

Effect 1	Effect 2

(ii)   He paid an initial rental of £2,500 by cheque for the shop that he is to trade from

Effect 1	Effect 2

(iii)   He purchased a van by cheque for £7,400

Effect 1	Effect 2

(iv)   He purchased £6,000 of goods for resale on credit

Effect 1	Effect 2

(v)   He sold goods for £1,000 – the customer paid by cheque

Effect 1	Effect 2

(vi)   He sold goods on credit for £4,800

Effect 1	Effect 2

(vii)   He paid shop assistants' wages by cheque totalling £2,100

Effect 1	Effect 2

(viii)   He made further sales on credit for £3,900

Effect 1	Effect 2

(ix) He purchased a further £1,400 of goods for resale by cheque

Effect 1	Effect 2

(x) £3,700 was received from credit customers

Effect 1	Effect 2

(xi) He paid £3,300 to credit suppliers

Effect 1	Effect 2

(xii) He withdrew £800 from the business for his living expenses

Effect 1	Effect 2

Task 6.4

Using the information above about James's early transactions, enter them into the given ledger accounts.

Bank

Details	£	Details	£

Capital

Details	£	Details	£

Rent

Details	£	Details	£

Van

Details	£	Details	£

Purchases

Details	£	Details	£

Purchases ledger control

Details	£	Details	£

Sales account

Details	£	Details	£

Sales ledger control

Details	£	Details	£

Wages

Details	£	Details	£

Drawings

Details	£	Details	£

Task 6.5

What is the double entry required for discounts allowed to customers?

	Debit ✓	Credit ✓
Discounts allowed		
Sales ledger control		

Task 6.6

Given below are two credit customers' accounts.

You are required to find the balance carried down on each account.

T N Designs			
	£		£
1 May balance b/d	2,643.56	8 May CB	1,473.28
11 May SDB – 27491	828.40	24 May SRDB Cn0381	256.89
18 May SDB – 27513	1,088.65		

Harold & partners			
	£		£
1 May balance b/d	1,367.83	7 MAY CB	635.78
5 May SDB – 27465	998.20	7 May CB – discount	33.46
12 May SDB – 27499	478.92	15 May SRDB – Cn0364	106.34
20 May SDB – 27524	258.28	30 May CB	663.66
		30 May CB – discount	34.93

Task 6.7

A payment is made to a supplier for £367.48 after a settlement discount of £12.50 has been taken.

What is the double entry for this transaction?

Account name	Debit £	Credit £

Task 6.8

For each of the following, indicate whether they are capital or revenue transactions:

	Capital ✓	Revenue ✓
Purchase of a new computer paid for by cheque		
Purchase of computer disks by cheque		
Purchase of a new business car on credit		
Payment of road tax on a new business car		
Payment of rent for the business premises		

Task 6.9

Calculate the balance on the following ledger accounts and bring them down, including appropriate dates, details and amounts.

Purchases ledger control

Date	Details	£	Date	Details	£
31 Oct	Purchases returns	4,467	1 Oct	Balance b/d	41,204
31 Oct	Bank	36,409	31 Oct	Purchases	52,390
31 Oct	Discounts received	125			

Petty cash

Date	Details	£	Date	Details	£
1 Oct	Balance b/d	200.00	31 Oct	Expenses	183.25
31 Oct	Bank	183.25			

VAT

Date	Details	£	Date	Details	£
31 Oct	Sales returns	40.00	1 Oct	Balance b/d	183.25
31 Oct	Purchases	1,900.00	31 Oct	Purchases returns	62.00
			31 Oct	Sales	3,250.00

Task 6.10

For each of the following, indicate whether they are capital or revenue transactions:

	Capital ✓	Revenue ✓
Payment of a credit supplier for goods received for resale		
Receipt of proceeds from sale of car used in the business		
Payment of drawings to the business owner		
Acquisition of new machine for use over five years		
Payment by a cash customer for goods		

Chapter 7

Task 7.1

James give you of the details of his sales on credit and receipts from credit customers during the first month (January 20XX). James is registered for VAT and charges VAT on all sales. He does not offer any discounts for early settlement.

Sales:			
Customer	Customer code	Invoice number	Invoice total £
To H Simms	SL 45	0001	1,800
To P Good	SL 21	0002	3,000
To K Mitchell	SL 30	0003	912
To C Brown	SL 05	0004	2,790

Receipts:	
Customer	£
From H Simms	900
From P Good	1,400
From K Mitchell	912
From C Brown	490

Record these transactions in the day books given and then post the day books to the general ledger accounts and the sales ledger.

Sales day book

Date 20XX	Customer	Invoice number	Customer code	Total £	VAT £	Net £

Cash book

Date	Details	Total £	VAT £	Cash sales £	Sales ledger £

General ledger

Sales ledger control

Details	£	Details	£

Sales

Details	£	Details	£

VAT

Details	£	Details	£

Sales ledger

H Simms SL 45

Details	£	Details	£

P Good SL 21

Details	£	Details	£

K Mitchell SL 30

Details	£	Details	£

C Brown SL 05

Details	£	Details	£

Task 7.2

Natural Productions is a small business that manufactures a variety of soaps and bath products which it sells directly to shops.

You are required to:

(a) **Post the totals of the sales day book to the general ledger accounts given**

(b) **Post the individual entries to the sales ledger**

Sales day book

Date 20XX	Customer	Invoice number	Total £	VAT £	Net £
2 Jan	Hoppers Ltd	6237	656.40	109.40	547.00
5 Jan	Body Perfect	6238	744.00	124.00	620.00
6 Jan	Esporta Leisure	6239	415.20	69.20	346.00
9 Jan	Langans Beauty	6240	273.60	45.60	228.00
12 Jan	Body Perfect	6241	657.60	109.60	548.00
16 Jan	Superior Products	6242	265.20	44.20	221.00
18 Jan	Esporta Leisure	6243	499.20	83.20	416.00
23 Jan	Hoppers Ltd	6244	285.60	47.60	238.00
26 Jan	Langans Beauty	6245	328.80	54.80	274.00
			4,125.60	687.60	3,438.00

(a) **General ledger**

Sales ledger control

Details	£	Details	£

VAT

Details	£	Details	£

Sales

Details	£	Details	£

(b) **Sales ledger**

Hoppers Ltd

Details	£	Details	£

Body Perfect

Details	£	Details	£

Esporta Leisure

Details	£	Details	£

Langans Beauty

Details	£	Details	£

Superior Products

Details	£	Details	£

Task 7.3

Given below are four sales invoices sent out by Short Furniture, a business that manufactures wooden garden furniture for sale to retail outlets. These are the only invoices that have been issued this week.

You are required to:

(a) **Enter the invoices into the sales day book given**

(b) **Total and check the sales day book**

(c) **Post the sales day book to the general ledger and the sales ledger**

INVOICE

Short Furniture
Eridge Estate
Benham DR6 4QQ
Tel 0303312 Fax 0303300
VAT Reg 0361 3282 60

To: Rocks Garden Suppliers
14 Windmill Lane
Benham

Invoice number: 08663

Date/tax point: 5 Jan 20XX

Order number: 4513

Account number: SL 22

Quantity	Description	Stock code	Unit amount £	Total £
2	6 Seat Dining Table	DT613	344.00	688.00
	Trade Discount			103.20

Net total		584.80
VAT		116.96
Invoice total		701.76

Terms
Net 30 days
E & OE

INVOICE

Short Furniture
Eridge Estate
Benham DR6 4QQ
Tel 0303312 Fax 0303300
VAT Reg 0361 3282 60

To: Eridge Nurseries
Eridge Estate
Benham

Invoice number: 08664

Date/tax point: 7 Jan 20XX

Order number: 61735F

Account number: SL 07

Quantity	Description	Stock code	Unit amount £	Total £
15	Plant Stands	PL006	23.85	357.75

Net total	357.75
VAT	71.55
Invoice total	429.30

Terms
Net 30 days
E & OE

INVOICE

Short Furniture
Eridge Estate
Benham DR6 4QQ
Tel 0303312 Fax 0303300
VAT Reg 0361 3282 60

To: Abergaven Garden Centre
Drenchley

Invoice number: 08665

Date/tax point: 7 Jan 20XX

Order number: S129

Account number: SL 16

Quantity	Description	Stock code	Unit amount £	Total £
3	Lounger Chairs	LC400	285.00	855.00
	Trade discount			85.50

Net total	769.50
VAT	153.90
Invoice total	923.40

Terms
Net 30 days
E & OE

INVOICE

Short Furniture
Eridge Estate
Benham DR6 4QQ
Tel 0303312 Fax 0303300
VAT Reg 0361 3282 60

To: Rother Nurseries
Rother Road
Benham

Invoice number: 08666

Date/tax point: 9 Jan 20XX

Order number: 06112

Account number: SL 13

Quantity	Description	Stock code	Unit amount £	Total £
2	Coffee Table	CT002	96.00	192.00
6	Dining Chairs	DC416	73.00	438.00
	Net total			630.00
	VAT			126.00
	Invoice total			756.00

Terms
Net 30 days
E & OE

(a) **Sales day book**

Customer	Invoice number	Customer code	Invoice total £	VAT £	Net £

(b) **Cross-cast check**

	£
Net	
VAT	____
Invoice total	====

(c) **General ledger**

Sales ledger control

Details	£	Details	£

VAT

Details	£	Details	£

Sales

Details	£	Details	£

Sales ledger

Eridge Nurseries   **SL 07**

Details	£	Details	£

Rother Nurseries   **SL 13**

Details	£	Details	£

Abergaven Garden Centre   SL 16

Details	£	Details	£

Rock Garden Supplies   SL 22

Details	£	Details	£

Task 7.4

Returning to Natural Productions (see Task 7.2), during January the company issued some credit notes.

You are required to:

(a) **Post the totals of the sales returns day book to the general ledger accounts given**

(b) **Post the individual entries to the sales ledger accounts used in the earlier task**

Sales returns day book

Date 20XX	Customer	Invoice number	Total £	VAT £	Net £
17 Jan	Hoppers Ltd	1476	82.44	13.74	68.70
23 Jan	Esporta Leisure	1477	107.04	17.84	89.20
30 Jan	Superior Products	1478	14.16	2.36	11.80
			203.64	33.94	169.70

(a) **General ledger**

Sales ledger control

Details	£	Details	£
Sales	4,125.60		

VAT

Details	£	Details	£
		Sales	687.60

Sales returns

Details	£	Details	£

(b) **Sales ledger**

Hoppers Ltd

Details	£	Details	£
SDB – 6237	656.40		
SDB – 6244	285.60		

Body Perfect

Details	£	Details	£
SDB – 6238	744.00		
SDB – 6241	657.60		

Esporta Leisure

Details	£	Details	£
SDB – 6239	415.20		
SDB – 6243	499.20		

Langans Beauty

Details	£	Details	£
SDB – 6240	273.60		
SDB – 6245	328.80		

Superior Products

Details	£	Details	£
SDB – 6242	265.20		

Task 7.5

Short Furniture has received the following remittance advices through the post in the week ending 7 February 20XX. The remittance advices from Rocks Garden Supplies and Eridge Nurseries were the ones sent out by Short Furniture with the monthly statement. However, the remittance advices from Abergaven Garden Centre and Rother Nurseries were prepared by their accounts departments and must therefore be checked to their accounts in the sales ledger, which are given below.

Check each payment thoroughly and record any problems or comments in the table provided.

Sales ledger

Rother Nurseries   SL 16

Date Details	£	Date Details	£
9 Jan SDB – 08666	756.00	20 Jan SRDB – 1470	96.50
16 Jan SDB – 08674	214.78		
24 Jan SDB – 08681	337.89		
5 Feb SDB – 08695	265.98		

Abergaven Garden Centre   SL 17

Date Details	£	Date Details	£
7 Jan SDB – 08665	923.40		
13 Jan SDB – 08672	623.56		
26 Jan SDB – 08685	316.58		
3 Feb SDB – 08692	415.76		

	Comments
Payment from Rocks Garden Supplies	
Payment from Eridge Nurseries	
Payment from Abergaven Garden Centre	
Payment from Rother Nurseries	

REMITTANCE ADVICE

To: Short Furniture
Eridge Estate
Benham DR6 4QQ
Tel 0303312 Fax 0303300

From: Rocks Garden Supplies

Date: 4 February 20XX

Reference	Amount £	Paid (✔)
08663	701.76	✔
1468	(343.57)	✔
08675	521.18	✔
08686	732.40	

CHEQUE ENCLOSED	£773.75

REMITTANCE ADVICE

To: Short Furniture
Eridge Estate
Benham DR6 4QQ
Tel 0303312 Fax 0303300

From: Eridge Nurseries

Date: 3 February 20XX

Reference	Amount £	Paid (✔)
08664	429.30	✔
08676	381.18	✔
1471	(206.23)	✔
08687	640.20	
08690	381.62	

CHEQUE ENCLOSED	£604.25

REMITTANCE ADVICE

To: Short Furniture
Eridge Estate
Benham DR6 4QQ
Tel 0303312 Fax 0303300

From: Abergaven Garden
Centre

Date: 4 February 20XX

Reference	Amount £	Paid (✓)
08665	923.40	✓
08672	623.56	✓
08685	316.58	✓

CHEQUE ENCLOSED	£1,863.54

REMITTANCE ADVICE

To: Short Furniture
Eridge Estate
Benham DR6 4QQ
Tel 0303312 Fax 0303300

From: Rother Nurseries

Date: 5 February 20XX

Reference	Amount £	Paid (✓)
08666	756.00	✓
08674	114.78	✓
1470	(96.50)	✓
08681	337.89	✓

CHEQUE ENCLOSED	£1,112.17

Task 7.6

Returning to Natural Productions (see Task 7.4) you are required to:

(i) Post the totals of receipts in the cash book to the general ledger accounts given below (note that in each case the discount was allowed to the customer after the invoice was prepared, and has been correctly calculated)

(ii) Post each individual receipt from customers to their account in the sales ledger given below

Date	Details	Total £	VAT £	Discounts allowed £	Cash sales £	Sales ledger £
23 Jan	Hoppers Ltd	553.96		20.00		553.96
23 Jan	Superior Products	116.70				116.70
24 Jan	Cash sales	131.16	21.86		109.30	
25 Jan	Esporta Leisure	367.20		11.36		367.20
27 Jan	Cash sales	88.56	14.76		73.80	
27 Jan	Body Perfect	706.64		21.86		706.64
27 Jan	Cash sales	60.12	10.02		50.10	
27 Jan	Langans Beauty	273.60	___	___	___	273.60
		2,297.94	46.64	53.22	233.20	2,018.10

General ledger

Bank

Details	£	Details	£

Sales ledger control

Details	£	Details	£
Sales	4,125.60	Sales returns	203.64

Sales

Details	£	Details	£
		SLCA	3,438.00

VAT

Details	£	Details	£
Sales returns	33.94	Sales	687.60

Discounts allowed

Details	£	Details	£

Sales ledger

Hoppers Ltd

Details	£	Details	£
SDB – 6237	656.40	SRDB – 1476	82.44
SDB – 6244	285.60		

Body Perfect

Details	£		£
SDB – 6238	744.00		
SDB – 6241	657.60		

Esporta Leisure

Details	£	Details	£
SDB – 6239	415.20	SRDB – 1477	107.04
SDB – 6243	499.20		

Langans Beauty

Details	£	Details	£
SDB – 6240	273.60		
SDB – 6245	328.80		

Superior Products

Details	£	Details	£
SDB – 6242	265.20	SRDB – 1478	14.16

Task 7.7

Ken trades in exotic dress materials. The following is a summary of his transactions with Crowley Ltd, a new credit customer.

£627 re invoice 1540 of 15 September
£728 re invoice 1560 of 29 September
£46 re credit note 89 of 3 October
£1,209 re invoice 1580 of 10 October
Cheque for £581 received 15 October

Complete the statement of account below.

Ken's Exotics
1 Bath Street
Cembury, CE11 9SD

To: Crowley Ltd

Date: 31 October 20XX

Date 20XX	Details	Transaction amount £	Outstanding amount £

Chapter 8

Task 8.1

For Natural Productions you are required to:

(a) **Post the totals of the purchases day book to the general ledger accounts given**

(b) **Post the individual entries to the purchases ledger accounts given**

Purchases day book

Date	Supplier	Invoice number	Total £	VAT £	Purchases £	Stationery £	Packaging £
4 Jan	P J Phillips	03576	428.40	71.40	357.00		
6 Jan	Trenter Ltd	18435	513.60	85.60	428.00		
9 Jan	W J Jones	43654	252.00	42.00		210.00	
12 Jan	P J Phillips	03598	495.60	82.60	413.00		
16 Jan	Packing Supplies	28423	321.60	53.60			268.00
19 Jan	Trenter Ltd	18478	625.20	104.20	521.00		
20 Jan	O & P Ltd	84335	748.80	124.80	624.00		
24 Jan	Packing Supplies	28444	196.80	32.80			164.00
28 Jan	Trenter Ltd	18491	441.60	73.60	368.00		
31 Jan	W J Jones	43681	124.80	20.80		104.00	
			4,148.40	691.40	2,711.00	314.00	432.00

General ledger

Purchases ledger control

Details	£	Details	£

VAT

Details	£	Details	£

Purchases

Details	£	Details	£

Stationery

Details	£	Details	£

Packaging

Details	£	Details	£

Purchases ledger

P J Phillips

Details	£	Details	£

Trenter Ltd

Details	£	Details	£

O & P Ltd

Details	£	Details	£

W J Jones

Details	£	Details	£

Packing Supplies

Details	£	Details	£

....

Task 8.2

Given below are the only four purchase invoices received by Short Furniture in the week ending 27 January 20XX. You are also given an extract from the supplier codes listing.

27 Jan Invoice No. 09642 from Ephraim Supplies £291.00 plus VAT for wood
27 Jan Invoice No. 06932 from Cavendish Woods £705.10 plus VAT for wood
27 Jan Invoice No. 67671 from Calverley Bros £145.60 plus VAT for polish
27 Jan Invoice No. 36004 from Culverden & Co £57.40 plus VAT for other purchases

Supplier codes listing

Calverley Bros	PL03
Cavendish Woods	PL14
Culverden & Co	PL23
Ephraim Supplies	PL39

You are required to:

(a) **Enter the invoices in the purchases day book given – note that purchases are analysed into wood, polish and varnish and other**

(b) **Total and check the purchases day book**

(c) **Post the purchases day book totals to the general ledger accounts given**

(d) **Post the individual entries in the purchases day book to the supplier's accounts in the purchases ledger given below**

Purchases day book

Date	Supplier	Invoice number	Supplier code	Total £	VAT £	Net £	Wood Purchases £	Polish/ varnish purchases £	Other purchases £

Cross cast check:

	£
Net	
VAT	
Total	

General ledger

Purchases ledger control

Details	£	Details	£

VAT

Details	£	Details	£

Wood purchases

Details	£	Details	£

Polish/varnish purchases

Details	£	Details	£

Other purchases

Details	£	Details	£

Purchases ledger

Carverley Bros   PL 03

Details	£	Details	£

Cavendish Woods   PL 03

Details	£	Details	£

Culverder & Co   PL 23

Details	£	Details	£

Ephraim Supplies   PL 39

Details	£	Details	£

··

Task 8.3

Returning to Natural Productions (see Task 8.1) you are required to:

(a) **Post the totals of the purchases returns day book to the general ledger accounts given**

(b) **Post the individual entries to the purchases ledger accounts also given below**

Purchases returns day book

Date	Supplier	Credit note number	Total £	VAT £	Purchases £	Stationery £	Packaging £
10 Jan	P J Phillips	04216	117.60	19.60	98.00		
16 Jan	W J Jones	CN0643	67.20	11.20		56.00	
30 Jan	O & P Ltd	CN1102	148.80	24.80	124.00		
			333.60	55.60	222.00	56.00	

General ledger

Purchases ledger control

Details	£	Details	£
		Purchases etc	4,148.40

VAT

Details	£	Details	£
Purchases etc	691.40		

Purchases returns

Details	£	Details	£

Stationery

Details	£	Details	£
PLCA	314.00		

Purchases ledger

P J Phillips

Details	£	Details	£
		PDB 03576	428.40
		PDB 03598	495.60

W J Jones

Details	£	Details	£
		PDB 43654	252.00
		PDB 43681	124.80

O & P Ltd

Details	£	Details	£
		PDB 84335	748.80

Task 8.4

You work for Natural Productions and one of your duties is to transfer data from the cash book to the ledgers. Most of the payments are to credit suppliers but there are some cash purchases of materials from small suppliers which include VAT.

You are required to:

(a) **Post the totals of the credit side of the cash book to the general ledger accounts given below**

(b) **Post each of the individual payments to the suppliers' accounts in the purchases ledger given below**

Cash book – credit side

Date	Details	Cheque No	Total £	VAT £	Discounts received £	Cash purchases £	Purchases ledger £
23 Jan	Trenter Ltd	002144	1,105.07		10.00		1,105.07
23 Jan	Cash purchase	002145	108.00	18.00		90.00	
24 Jan	W J Jones	002146	252.00				252.00
24 Jan	P J Phillips	002147	806.40				806.40
24 Jan	Cash purchase	002148	128.28	21.38		106.90	
25 Jan	Packing Supp	002149	309.90		5.00		309.90
26 Jan	O & P Ltd	002150	580.00		20.00		580.00
27 Jan	Cash purchase	002151	96.96	16.16		80.80	
			3,386.61	55.54	35.00	277.70	3,053.37

General ledger

Purchases ledger control

Details	£	Details	£
Purchases returns etc	333.60	Purchases etc	4,148.40

VAT

Details	£	Details	£
Purchases etc	691.40	Purchases returns etc	55.60

Purchases

Details	£	Details	£
PLCA	2,711.00		

Discounts received

Details	£	Details	£

Purchases ledger

P J Phillips

Details	£	Details	£
PRDB 04216	117.60	PDB 03576	428.40
		PDB 03598	495.60

Trenter Ltd

Details	£	Details	£
		PDB 18435	513.60
		PDB 18478	625.20
		PDB 18491	441.60

W J Jones

Details	£	Details	£
PRDB CN0643	67.20	PDB 43654	252.00
		PDB 43681	124.80

O & P Ltd

Details	£	Details	£
PRDB CN1102	148.80	PDB 84335	748.80

Packing Supplies

Details	£	Details	£
		PDB 28423	321.60
		PDB 28444	196.80

Task 8.5

Ken trades in exotic dress materials. The following is the credit side of Ken's Petty Cash Book, which acts only as a book of prime entry.

(a) **What will be the FIVE entries in the general ledger?**

Petty cash book – credit side

Details	Voucher number	Total £	VAT £	Office expenses £	Stationery £	Maintenance £
Tea, coffee and milk for office	1234	15.20		15.20		
Printer cartridge	1235	39.12	6.52		32.60	
Repair to fire extinguisher	1236	54.00	9.00			45.00
Totals		108.32	15.52	15.20	32.60	45.00

General ledger

Account name	Amount £	Debit ✓	Credit ✓

(b) **Which entry would be omitted if Ken's Petty Cash Book operated as a general ledger account as well?**

Task 8.6

Ken trades in exotic dress materials. He codes all purchase invoices with a supplier code AND a general ledger code. A selection of the codes used is given below.

Supplier	Supplier Code
Henderson Co	HEN562
Mack Materials	MAC930
Vinceroy Ltd	VIN234
Streamers	STR220
AVR Partners	AVR001

Product	General Ledger Code
Lace	GL501
Calico	GL502
Seersucker	GL503
Cambric	GL504
Velvet	GL505

This is an invoice received from a supplier.

Vinceroy Ltd **17 Fall Road, Agburton AG5 2WE** **VAT Registration No. 783 2873 33** **Invoice number: 892**	
Ken's Exotics 1 Bath Street Cembury, CE11 9SD	5 Feb 20XX
20 metres .... Velvet @ £7.00 per metre	£140.00
VAT @ 20%	£ 28.00
Total	£168.00

(a) **Select which codes would be used to code this invoice.**

Supplier account code	
General ledger code	

(b) **Why is it necessary to use a general ledger code?**

Picklist:

To help trace relevant accounts quickly and easily
To make sure the correct balances are calculated
To prevent fraud

Chapter 9

Task 9.1

You are given the following account balances from the general ledger of your organisation.

Would each balance be a debit or a credit balance in the trial balance?

Ledger account	Balance	Debit ✓	Credit ✓
Sales	592,513		
Telephone	1,295		
Sales ledger control	52,375		
Wages	104,288		
Purchases returns	8,229		
Bank overdraft	17,339		
Purchases	372,589		
Drawings	71,604		
Sales returns	32,800		
Car	14,700		
Purchases ledger control	31,570		

Task 9.2

Given below is the list of ledger balances for your organisation at 31 January 20XX.

You are required to prepare a trial balance as at 31 January 20XX.

	£	Debit £	Credit £
Motor vehicles	76,800		
Office equipment	36,440		
Sales	285,600		
Purchases	196,800		
Bank overdraft	2,016		
Petty cash	36		
Capital	90,000		
Sales returns	5,640		
Purchases returns	4,320		
Sales ledger control	42,960		
Purchases ledger control	36,120		
VAT owed to HMRC	15,540		
Drawings	12,040		
Telephone	1,920		
Electricity	3,360		
Wages	74,520		
Loan from bank	36,000		
Discounts allowed	7,680		
Discounts received	4,680		
Rent expense	16,080		
Totals			

Task 9.3

The double-entry system of bookkeeping normally results in which of the following balances on the ledger accounts?

✓	Debit balances	Credit balances
	Assets and income	Liabilities, capital and expenses
	Income, capital and liabilities	Assets and expenses
	Assets and expenses	Liabilities, capital and income
	Assets, expenses and capital	Liabilities and income

Task 9.4

A credit balance on a ledger account indicates

✓	
	An asset or an expense
	A liability or an expense
	An amount owing to the organisation
	A liability or income

Task 9.5

Which of the following balances would be a credit balance on a trial balance?

✓	
	Non-current assets
	Sales returns
	Discounts allowed
	Bank overdraft

Task 9.6

Given below is the list of ledger balances for your organisation at 31 August.

You are required to prepare a trial balance as at 31 August.

	£	Debit £	Credit £
Bank overdraft	4,838		
Capital	216,000		
Discounts allowed	18,432		
Discounts received	11,232		
Drawings	28,896		
Electricity	8,064		
Loan from bank	86,400		
Motor vehicles	184,320		
Office equipment	87,456		
Petty cash	100		
Purchases	472,320		
Purchases ledger control	86,688		
Purchases returns	10,368		
Rent expense	38,592		
Sales	685,440		
Sales ledger control	103,104		
Sales returns	13,536		
Telephone	4,608		
VAT owed to HMRC	37,310		
Wages	178,848		
Totals			

Answer bank

Answer bank

BPP
LEARNING MEDIA

Basic Accounting I Answer bank

Chapter 1

Task 1.1

	Cash transaction ✓	Credit transaction ✓
Purchase of goods for £200 payable by cash in one week's time		✓
Writing a cheque for the purchase of a new computer	✓	
Sale of goods to a customer where the invoice accompanies the goods		✓
Receipt of a cheque from a customer for goods purchased today	✓	
Purchase of goods where payment is due in three weeks' time		✓

Task 1.2

The correct answer is: an invoice

Task 1.3

The correct answer is: an alpha-numeric system

Chapter 2

Task 2.1

The correct answer is: a trade discount

Task 2.2

The correct answer is: HM Revenue and Customs

Task 2.3

Goods total	Trade discount (15% × price) £	Net total £
£416.80	62.52	354.28
£105.60	15.84	89.76
£96.40	14.46	81.94
£263.20	39.48	223.72
£351.00	52.65	298.35

Task 2.4

Net total	VAT (Net × 20%) £	Invoice total £
£258.90	51.78	310.68
£316.80	63.36	380.16
£82.60	16.52	99.12
£152.70	30.54	183.24
£451.30	90.26	541.56

Task 2.5

Net total	VAT (Note) £	Invoice total £
£258.90	50.22	309.12
£316.80	61.45	378.25
£82.60	16.02	98.62
£152.70	29.62	182.32
£451.30	87.55	538.85

Note: The VAT is calculated on the net total **after** deducting the settlement discount:

(Net total − (Net total × 3%)) × 20/100. The VAT amount is always rounded **down** to the nearest penny.

Task 2.6

Invoice total £	VAT (Invoice total × 20/120) £	Net total £
145.20	24.20	121.00
66.90	11.15	55.75
246.60	41.10	205.50
35.40	5.90	29.50
125.40	20.90	104.50

Task 2.7

Invoice total £	VAT (Invoice total × 20/120) £	Net total £
252.66	42.11	210.55
169.20	28.20	141.00
48.60	8.10	40.50
104.28	17.38	86.90
60.48	10.08	50.40
822.60	137.10	685.50

Chapter 3

Task 3.1

The correct answer is £120 (100 + (100 × 20/100) = 120)

Task 3.2

The correct answer is £108 ((100 − (100 × 10/100)) = 90 + (90 × 20/100) = 108)

Task 3.3

Sales day book

Customer	Invoice number	Invoice total £	VAT £	Net £
Hoppers Ltd	6237	656.40	109.40	547.00
Body Perfect	6238	744.00	124.00	620.00
Esporta Leisure	6239	415.20	69.20	346.00
Langans Beauty	6240	273.60	45.60	228.00
Body Perfect	6241	657.60	109.60	548.00
Superior Products	6242	265.20	44.20	221.00
Esporta Leisure	6243	499.20	83.20	416.00
Hoppers Ltd	6244	285.60	47.60	238.00
Langans Beauty	6245	328.80	54.80	274.00
		4,125.60	687.60	3,438.00

Cross-cast check:

	£
Net	3,438.00
VAT	687.60
Invoice total	4,125.60

Task 3.4

Sales returns day book

Customer	Credit note number	Credit note total £	VAT £	Net £
Hoppers Ltd	1476	82.44	13.74	68.70
Esporta Leisure	1477	107.04	17.84	89.20
Superior Products	1478	14.10	2.35	11.75
		203.58	33.93	169.65

Cross-cast check:

	£
Net	169.65
VAT	33.93
Invoice total	203.58

Task 3.5

Purchases day book

Date	Supplier	Invoice number	Invoice total £	VAT £	Purchases (materials) £	Stationery £	Packaging £
4 Jan	P J Phillips	03576	428.40	71.40	357.00		
6 Jan	Trenter Ltd	18435	513.60	85.60	428.00		
9 Jan	W J Jones	43654	252.00	42.00		210.00	
12 Jan	P J Phillips	03598	495.60	82.60	413.00		
16 Jan	Packing Supplies	28423	321.60	53.60			268.00
19 Jan	Trenter Ltd	18478	625.20	104.20	521.00		
20 Jan	O & P Ltd	84335	748.80	124.80	624.00		
24 Jan	Packing Supplies	28444	196.80	32.80			164.00
28 Jan	Trenter Ltd	18491	441.60	73.60	368.00		
31 Jan	W J Jones	43681	124.80	20.80		104.00	
			4,148.40	691.40	2,711.00	314.00	432.00

Cross-cast check:

	£
Packaging	432.00
Stationery	314.00
Purchases (materials)	2,711.00
VAT	691.40
Invoice total	4,148.40

Task 3.6

Purchases returns day book

Date	Supplier	Credit note number	Credit note total £	VAT £	Purchases (materials) £	Stationery £	Packaging £
10 Jan	P J Phillips	04216	117.60	19.60	98.00		
16 Jan	W J Jones	0643	67.20	11.20		56.00	
30 Jan	O & P Ltd	1102	148.80	24.80	124.00		
			333.60	55.60	222.00	56.00	

Cross-cast check:

	£
Packaging	0.00
Stationery	56.00
Purchases (materials)	222.00
VAT	55.60
Credit note total	333.60

Chapter 4

Task 4.1

The correct answer is: a price list

....

Task 4.2

The correct answer is: allocate one of two sales codes to each invoice and use this to write up the invoices in the analysed sales day book.

....

Task 4.3

INVOICE number		57104		
Southfield Electrical, Industrial Estate, Benham DR6 2FF				
VAT registration:		0264 2274 49		
Date/tax point:		8/1/XX		
Order number:		32431		
Customer:		Whitehill Superstores		
Account number (customer code)		SL 44		
Product code		Quantity	Unit amount £	Total £
6060		8	300.00	2,400.00
Trade discount	10	%		240.00
Net total				2,160.00
VAT at 20%				414.72
Invoice total				2,574.72
Settlement discount			4	%

INVOICE number	57105		
Southfield Electrical, Industrial Estate, Benham DR6 2FF			
VAT registration:	0264 2274 49		
Date/tax point:	8/1/XX		
Order number:	24316		
Customer name:	Quinn Ltd		
Account number (customer code)	SL 04		
Product code	Quantity	Unit amount £	Total £
3170	14	35.00	490.00
Trade discount 15	%		73.50
Net total			416.50
VAT at 20%			83.30
Invoice total			499.80
Settlement discount		0	%

INVOICE number	57106		
Southfield Electrical, Industrial Estate, Benham DR6 2FF			
VAT registration:	0264 2274 49		
Date/tax point:	8/1/XX		
Order number:	04367		
Customer:	Harper & Sons		
Account number (customer code)	SL 26		
Product code	Quantity	Unit amount £	Total £
6150	3	260.00	780.00
Trade discount 10	%		78.00
Net total			702.00
VAT at 20%			136.18
Invoice total			838.18
Settlement discount		3	%

···

Task 4.4

The invoice is for 15 toasters (as ordered) whereas the delivery note shows that only 12 were delivered – the invoice should be amended to show only 12 toasters and the reason for the short delivery should be investigated.

The invoice is charging the vacuums at £220 each whereas the purchase order shows a unit price of £210 – this difference should be investigated – was it agreed in a price quotation to Whitehill that the price would be only £210?

···

Task 4.5

Errors on the credit note:

- The calculation of the total for the whisks is incorrect.
- The trade discount has been omitted.
- The VAT has been rounded up (not down) and has been deducted rather than added.

Corrected figures:

	£
Fridges	660.00
Whisks (2 × £6.99)	13.98
	673.98
Less: 20% trade discount (rounded up to nearest penny)	(134.80)
Net total	539.18
VAT (rounded down to nearest penny)	107.83
Invoice total	647.01

....

Task 4.6

(a) and (b)

Date	Customer	Credit note number	Customer code	Credit note total £	VAT £	Net £
21/9	Whitehill Superstores	08650	SL 44	356.40	59.40	297.00
23/9	Dagwell Enterprises	08651	SL 15	244.80	40.80	204.00
	Totals			601.20	100.20	501.00

....

Task 4.7

Sales ledger

Alpha Services   **SL 10**

Details	£	Details	£
Balance b/d	253.63	SRDB – 551	624.00
SDB – 715	5,190.00	CB – 013278	253.63
SDB – 787	10,020.00		

STATEMENT OF ACCOUNT	
Southfield Electrical	
Industrial Estate	
Benham DR6 2FF	
Tel: 01239 345639	
VAT registration:	0264 2274 49
Date:	31 May 20XX
Customer:	Alpha Services 83 Abbey Road Durringham DU5 2WP
Account number (customer code)	SL 10

Date	Details	Debit £	Credit £	Balance £
1/5/XX	Bal b/d			253.63
2/5/XX Payment received – thank you			253.63	0.00
7/5/XX	Inv 715	5,190.00		5,190.00
12/5/XX	CN 551		624.00	4,566.00
17/5/XX	Inv 787	10,020.00		14,586.00
Amount now due				14,586.00

Task 4.8

Cheque from Hayworth Ltd – the settlement discount should not have been taken as the cheque arrived 13 days after the invoice date even though it was written only 9 days after the invoice date.

Cheque from Harper & Sons – a discount of £29.56 has been taken. The discount is valid but has been incorrectly calculated. The correct discount is £620.00 × 4/100 = £24.80. Therefore the cheque should have been made out for £739.04 – £24.80 = £714.24.

Chapter 5

Task 5.1

When a supplier delivers materials to him he retains the supplier's delivery note and also prepares a goods received note once he has had a chance to inspect the quality of the items.

Task 5.2

The correct answer is: a product code

Task 5.3

(a) The correct answer is: 20 June

(b) The correct answer is: £235.20

Workings

Discount: (239.20 – 39.20) × 2/100 = 4.00

Payment: 239.2 – 4.00 = 235.20

Task 5.4

Invoice date	Supplier name	Payment date	Working	Amount of cheque £
5 Jan	Henson Press	27 Jan		336.00
8 Jan	GH Publications	3 Feb		136.80
12 Jan	Ely Instruments	27 Jan	£640.00 – (2% × 640.00) + 125.44	752.64
15 Jan	Hams Instruments	10 Feb		370.45
19 Jan	CD Supplies	10 Feb		138.02

BPP
LEARNING MEDIA

Invoice date	Supplier name	Payment date	Working	Amount of cheque £
22 Jan	Jester Press	27 Jan	£127.60 – (3.5% × 127.60) + 24.62	147.75
22 Jan	Henson Press	17 Feb		306.00
23 Jan	CD Supplies	27 Jan	£65.40 – (3% × 65.40) + 12.68	76.12
25 Jan	Jester Press	27 Jan	£39.50 – (3.5% × 39.50) + 7.62	45.74
25 Jan	Buser Ltd	27 Jan	£245.00 – (5% × 245.00) + 46.55	279.30

Task 5.5

REMITTANCE ADVICE

To: P.T. Supplies
28 Farm Court Road
Drenchley DR22 4XT

From: Edgehill Designs

Date: 7 February 20XX

Reference	Amount £	Paid (✓)
20671	107.22	✓
20692	157.63	✓
CN 04722	(28.41)	✓

CHEQUE ENCLOSED	£236.44

Task 5.6

- The invoice quantity agrees to the purchase order but the delivery note and GRN show that only 6 tumble dryers were delivered.

- The calculation of the total cost of the tumble dryers is incorrect. It should be £1,715 (7 × £245) not £1,778.

- The VAT calculation is incorrect – it should be:

	£
Net total	1,821.42
Less: settlement discount (£1,821.42 × 4/100)	(72.86)
	1,748.56
VAT £1,748.56 × 20/100 (rounded down)	349.71

Task 5.7

- No trade discount has been deducted despite the supplier's file showing that a trade discount of 10% is normally deducted.

- The net total of the goods is incorrect and should total £2,508, not £2,535.

Task 5.8

Purchases day book

Date 20XX	Details	Invoice number	Total £	VAT £	Net £
30 June	Seashell Ltd	8971	3,788.98	577.98	3,211.00
30 June	Opal & Co	05119	4,800.00	800.00	4,000.00
	Totals		8,588.98	1,377.98	7,211.00

Purchases ledger

Account name	Amount £	Debit ✓	Credit ✓
Seashell Ltd	3,788.98		✓
Opal & Co	4,800.00		✓

Task 5.9

(a) The correct answer is: discount received £20

(b) The correct answer is: credit note 3215 £250

(c) The correct answer is: £723

Working

£743 – £20 = £723

....

Task 5.10

VAT: $((30 \times 20) - (30 \times 20 \times 10/100)) \times 20/100$

Total: $(30 \times 20) - (30 \times 20 \times 10/100) + 108.00$

	Yes ✓	No ✓
Has the correct purchase price of the cardboard boxes been charged?		✓
Has the correct discount been applied?		✓
What would be the VAT amount charged if the invoice was correct?	£	108.00
What would be the total amount charged if the invoice was correct?	£	648.00

....

Task 5.11

(a)

Ken's Exotics
1 Bath Street
Cembury, CE11 9SD

REMITTANCE ADVICE

To: Mack Materials   Date: 30 June 20XX

Please find attached our cheque in payment of the following amounts.

Invoice number	Credit note number	Amount £
901		760
	43	31
Total amount paid		729

(b) The correct answer is: the remittance advice note will be sent to the supplier to advise them of the amount being paid

Task 5.12

The correct answer is: Ken sent a cheque for £1,586 to the supplier on 30 June 20XX

Chapter 6

Task 6.1

	Asset ✓	Liability ✓
A trade receivable	✓	
A car used in the business	✓	
A loan from the bank		✓
A bank overdraft		✓
Cash in hand	✓	
VAT owed to HMRC		✓
A trade payable		✓

Task 6.2

An increase in an expense is a   debit
A decrease in a liability is a   debit
An increase in income is a   credit
An increase in an asset is a   debit
An increase in capital is a   credit
A decrease in an asset is a   credit
An increase in a liability is a   credit
A decrease in capital is a   debit

Task 6.3

(i) James paid £20,000 into a business bank account in order to start the business

Effect 1	Effect 2
Increase in cash	Increase in capital of business on set-up

(ii) He paid an initial rental of £2,500 by cheque for the shop that he is to trade from

Effect 1	Effect 2
Decrease in cash	Rent expense incurred

(iii) He purchased a van by cheque for £7,400

Effect 1	Effect 2
Decrease in cash	Increase in asset – the van

(iv) He purchased £6,000 of goods for resale on credit

Effect 1	Effect 2
Increase in purchases	Increase in trade payables

(v) He sold goods for £1,000 - the customer paid by cheque

Effect 1	Effect 2
Increase in cash	Increase in sales

(vi) He sold goods on credit for £4,800

Effect 1	Effect 2
Increase in trade receivables	Increase in sales

(vii) He paid shop assistants' wages by cheque totalling £2,100

Effect 1	Effect 2
Decrease in cash	Wages expense incurred

(viii) He made further sales on credit for £3,900

Effect 1	Effect 2
Increase in trade receivables	Increase in sales

(ix) He purchased a further £1,400 of goods for resale by cheque

Effect 1	Effect 2
Decrease in cash	Increase in purchases

(x) £3,700 was received from credit customers

Effect 1	Effect 2
Increase in cash	Decrease in trade receivables

(xi) He paid £3,300 to credit suppliers

Effect 1	Effect 2
Decrease in cash	Decrease in trade payables

(xii) He withdrew £800 from the business for his living expenses

Effect 1	Effect 2
Decrease in cash	Increase in drawings

Task 6.4

Bank

Details	£	Details	£
Capital (i)	20,000	Rent (ii)	2,500
Sales (v)	1,000	Van (iii)	7,400
Sales ledger control (x)	3,700	Wages (vii)	2,100
		Purchases (ix)	1,400
		Purchases ledger control (xi)	3,300
		Drawings (xii)	800

Capital

Details	£	Details	£
		Bank (i)	20,000

Rent

Details	£	Details	£
Bank (ii)	2,500		

Van

Details	£	Details	£
Bank (iii)	7,400		

Purchases

Details	£	Details	£
Purchases ledger control (iv)	6,000		
Bank (ix)	1,400		

Purchases ledger control

Details	£	Details	£
Bank (xi)	3,300	Purchases (iv)	6,000

Sales account

Details	£	Details	£
		Bank (v)	1,000
		Sales ledger control (vi)	4,800
		Sales ledger control (viii)	3,900

Sales ledger control

Details	£	Details	£
Sales (vi)	4,800	Bank (x)	3,700
Sales (viii)	3,900		

Wages

Details	£	Details	£
Bank (vii)	2,100		

Drawings

Details	£	Details	£
Bank (xii)	800		

Task 6.5

	Debit ✓	Credit ✓
Discounts allowed	✓	
Sales ledger control		✓

Task 6.6

T N Designs			
	£		£
1 May balance b/d	2,643.56	8 May CB	1,473.28
11 May SDB – 27491	828.40	24 May SRDB Cn0381	256.89
18 May SDB – 27513	1,088.65		2,828.44
	4,555.61		4,555.61

Harold & partners			
	£		£
1 May balance b/d	1,367.83	7 MAY CB	635.78
5 May SDB – 27465	998.20	7 May CB – discount	33.46
12 May SDB – 27499	478.92	15 May SRDB – Cn0364	106.34
20 May SDB – 27524	258.28	30 May CB	663.66
		30 May CB – discount	34.93
		31 May balance c/d	1,629.07
	3,103.24		3,103.24

Task 6.7

	Debit £	Credit £
Purchases ledger control	367.48	
Bank		367.48
Purchases ledger control	12.50	
Discount received		12.50

Task 6.8

	Capital ✓	Revenue ✓
Purchase of a new computer paid for by cheque	✓	
Purchase of computer disks by cheque		✓
Purchase of a new business car on credit	✓	
Payment of road tax on a new business car		✓
Payment of rent for the business premises		✓

Task 6.9

Purchases ledger control

Date	Details	£	Date	Details	£
31 Oct	Purchases returns	4,467	1 Oct	Balance b/d	41,204
31 Oct	Bank	36,409	31 Oct	Purchases	52,390
31 Oct	Discounts received	125			
31 Oct	Balance c/d	52,593			
		93,594			93,594
			1 Nov	Balance b/d	52,593

Petty cash

Date	Details	£	Date	Details	£
1 Oct	Balance b/d	200.00	31 Oct	Expenses	183.25
31 Oct	Bank	183.25	31 Oct	Balance c/d	200.00
		383.25			383.25
1 Nov	Balance b/d	200.00			

VAT

Date	Details	£	Date	Details	£
31 Oct	Sales returns	40.00	1 Oct	Balance b/d	183.25
31 Oct	Purchases	1,900.00	31 Oct	Purchases returns	62.00
31 Oct	Balance c/d	1,555.25	31 Oct	Sales	3.250.00
		3,495.25			3,495.25
			1 Nov	Balance b/d	1,555.25

Task 6.10

	Capital ✓	Revenue ✓
Payment of a credit supplier for goods received for resale		✓
Receipt of proceeds from sale of car used in the business	✓	
Payment of drawings to the business owner	✓	
Acquisition of new machine for use over five years	✓	
Payment by a cash customer for goods		✓

Chapter 7

Task 7.1

Sales day book

Date 20XX	Customer	Invoice number	Customer code	Total £	VAT (Total × 20/120) £	Net £
Jan	H Simms	0001	SL 45	1,800	300	1,500
Jan	P Good	0002	SL 21	3,000	500	2,500
Jan	K Mitchell	0003	SL 30	912	152	760
Jan	C Brown	0004	SL 05	2,790	465	2,325
Totals				8,502	1,417	7,085

Cash book

Date 20XX	Details	Total £	VAT £	Cash sales £	Sales ledger £
Jan	From H Simms	900.00			900.00
Jan	From P Good	1,400.00			1,400.00
Jan	From K Mitchell	912.00			912.00
Jan	From C Brown	490.00			490.00
Totals		3,702.00			3,702.00

General ledger

Sales ledger control

Details	£	Details	£
Sales	8,502.00	Bank	3,702.00

Sales

Details	£	Details	£
		SLCA	7,085.00

VAT

Details	£	Details	£
		Sales	1,417.00

Sales ledger

H Simms SL 45

Details	£	Details	£
SDB 0001	1,800.00	CB	900.00

P Good SL 21

Details	£	Details	£
SDB 0002	3,000.00	CB	1,400.00

K Mitchell SL 30

Details	£	Details	£
SDB 0003	912.00	CB	912.00

C Brown SL 05

Details	£	Details	£
SDB 0004	2,790.00	CB	490.00

Task 7.2

(a) General ledger

Sales ledger control

Details	£	Details	£
Sales	4,125.60		

VAT

Details	£	Details	£
		Sales	687.60

Sales

Details	£	Details	£
		SLCA	3,438.00

(b) Sales ledger

Hoppers Ltd

Details	£	Details	£
SDB 6237	656.40		
SDB 6244	285.60		

Body Perfect

Details	£	Details	£
SDB 6238	744.00		
SDB 6241	657.60		

Esporta Leisure

Details	£	Details	£
SDB 6239	415.20		
SDB 6243	499.20		

Langans Beauty

Details	£	Details	£
SDB 6240	273.60		
SDB 6245	328.80		

Superior Products

Details	£	Details	£
SDB 6242	265.20		

Task 7.3

Sales day book

Customer	Invoice number	Customer code	Invoice total £	VAT £	Net £
Rocks Garden Supplies	08663	SL22	701.76	116.96	584.80
Eridge Nurseries	08664	SL07	429.30	71.55	357.75
Abergaven GC	08665	SL16	923.40	153.90	769.50
Rother Nurseries	08666	SL13	756.00	126.00	630.00
			2,810.46	468.41	2,342.05

Cross-cast check:

	£
Net	2,342.05
VAT	468.41
Invoice total	2,810.46

General ledger

Sales ledger control

Details	£	Details	£
Sales	2,810.46		

VAT

Details	£	Details	£
		Sales	468.41

Sales

Details	£	Details	£
		SLCA	2,342.05

Sales ledger

Eridge Nurseries   SL 07

Details	£	Details	£
7 Jan SDB – 08664	429.30		

Rother Nurseries   SL 13

Details	£	Details	£
9 Jan SDB – 08666	756.00		

Abergaven Garden Centre   SL 16

Details	£	Details	£
7 Jan SDB – 08665	923.40		

Rocks Garden Centre   SL 22

Details	£	Details	£
5 Jan SDB – 08663	701.76		

Task 7.4

(a) **General ledger**

Sales ledger control

	£		£
Sales	4,125.60	Sales returns	203.64

VAT

	£		£
Sales returns	33.94	Sales	687.60

Sales returns

	£		£
SLCA	169.70		

(b) **Sales ledger**

Hoppers Ltd

	£		£
SDB – 6237	656.40	SRDB 1476	82.44
SDB – 6244	285.60		

Body Perfect

	£		£
SDB – 6238	744.00		
SDB – 6241	657.60		

Esporta Leisure

	£		£
SDB – 6239	415.20	SRDB 1477	107.04
SDB – 6243	499.20		

Langans Beauty

	£		£
SDB – 6240	273.60		
SDB – 6245	328.80		

Superior Products

	£		£
SDB – 6242	265.20	SRDB 1478	14.16

Task 7.5

	Comments
Payment from Rocks Garden Supplies	The remittance advice has been wrongly added up – the total should be £879.37
Payment from Eridge Nurseries	This is perfectly acceptable and valid
Payment from Abergaven Garden Centre	This is perfectly acceptable and valid
Payment from Rother Nurseries	On the remittance advice Rother Nurseries has recorded invoice 08674 as £114.78 rather than £214.78 – therefore the amount of the payment is wrong

Task 7.6

General ledger

Bank

Details	£	Details	£
Sales/VAT/SLCA	2,297.94		

Sales ledger control

Details	£	Details	£
Sales	4,125.60	Sales returns	203.64
		Bank	2,018.10
		Discounts allowed	53.22

Sales

Details	£	Details	£
		SLCA	3,438.00
		Bank	233.20

VAT

Details	£	Details	£
Sales returns	33.94	Sales	687.60
		Bank	46.64

Discounts allowed

Details	£	Details	£
SLCA	53.22		

Sales ledger

Hoppers Ltd

Details	£	Details	£
SDB – 6237	656.40	SRDB – 1476	82.44
SDB – 6244	285.60	CB	553.96
		CB – discount	20.00

Body Perfect

Details	£		£
SDB – 6238	744.00	CB	706.64
SDB – 6241	657.60	CB – discount	21.86

Esporta Leisure

Details	£	Details	£
SDB – 6239	415.20	SRDB – 1477	107.04
SDB – 6243	499.20	CB	367.20
		CB – discount	11.36

Langans Beauty

Details	£	Details	£
SDB – 6240	273.60	CB	273.60
SDB – 6245	328.80		

Superior Products

Details	£	Details	£
SDB – 6242	265.20	SRDB – 1478	14.16
		CB	116.70

Task 7.7

<table>
<tr><td colspan="4" align="center">Ken's Exotics
1 Bath Street
Cembury, CE11 9SD</td></tr>
<tr><td colspan="2">To: Crowley Ltd</td><td colspan="2" align="right">Date: 31 October 20XX</td></tr>
<tr><th>Date 20XX</th><th>Details</th><th>Transaction amount
£</th><th>Outstanding amount
£</th></tr>
<tr><td>15/9</td><td>Invoice 1540</td><td align="center">627</td><td align="center">627</td></tr>
<tr><td>29/9</td><td>Invoice 1560</td><td align="center">728</td><td align="center">1,355</td></tr>
<tr><td>3/10</td><td>Credit note 89</td><td align="center">(46)</td><td align="center">1,309</td></tr>
<tr><td>10/10</td><td>Invoice 1580</td><td align="center">1,209</td><td align="center">2,518</td></tr>
<tr><td>15/10</td><td>Cheque</td><td align="center">(581)</td><td align="center">1,937</td></tr>
</table>

Chapter 8

Task 8.1

Purchases ledger control

Details	£	Details	£
		Purchases etc	4,148.40

VAT

Details	£	Details	£
Purchases etc	691.40		

Purchases

Details	£	Details	£
PLCA	2,711.00		

Stationery

Details	£	Details	£
PLCA	314.00		

Packaging

Details	£	Details	£
PLCA	432.00		

Purchases ledger

P J Phillips

Details	£	Details	£
		PDB 03576	428.40
		PDB 03598	495.60

Trenter Ltd

Details	£	Details	£
		PDB 18435	513.60
		PDB 18478	625.20
		PDB 18491	441.60

W J Jones

Details	£	Details	£
		PDB 43654	252.00
		PDB 43681	124.80

O & P Ltd

Details	£	Details	£
		PDB 84335	748.80

Packing Supplies

Details	£	Details	£
		PDB 28423	321.60
		PDB 28444	196.80

··

Task 8.2

Purchases day book

Date	Supplier	Invoice number	Supplier code	Total £	VAT £	Net £	Wood purchases £	Polish/ varnish purchases £	Other purchases £
27 Jan	Ephraim Supplies	09642	PL39	349.20	58.20	291.00	291.00		
27 Jan	Cavendish Woods	06932	PL14	846.12	141.02	705.10	705.10		
27 Jan	Calverley Bros	67671	PL03	174.72	29.12	145.60		145.60	
27 Jan	Culverden & Co	36004	PL23	68.88	11.48	57.40			57.40
				1,438.92	239.82	1,199.10	996.10	145.60	57.40

Cross-cast check:

	£
Net	1,199.10
VAT	239.82
Total	1,438.92

General ledger

Purchases ledger control

Details	£		£
		Purchases	1,438.92

VAT

Details	£		£
Purchases	239.82		

Wood purchases

Details	£		£
PLCA	996.10		

Polish/varnish purchases

Details	£		£
PLCA	145.60		

Other purchases

Details	£		£
PLCA	57.40		

Purchases ledger

Calverley Bros   PL 03

Details	£		£
		PDB 67671	174.72

Cavendish Woods   PL 14

Details	£		£
		PDB 06932	846.12

Culverden & Co   PL 23

Details	£		£
		PDB 36004	68.88

Ephraim Supplies   PL 39

Details	£		£
		PDB 09642	349.20

Task 8.3

General ledger

Purchases ledger control

Details	£	Details	£
Purchases returns	333.60	Purchases etc	4,148.40

VAT

Details	£	Details	£
Purchases etc	691.40	Purchases returns	55.60

Purchases returns

Details	£	Details	£
		PLCA	222.00

Stationery

Details	£	Details	£
PLCA	314.00	PLCA	56.00

Purchases ledger

P J Phillips

Details	£	Details	£
PRDB 04216	117.60	PDB 03576	428.40
		PDB 03598	495.60

W J Jones

Details	£	Details	£
PRDB 0643	67.20	PDB 43654	252.00
		PDB 43681	124.80

O & P Ltd

Details	£	Details	£
PRDB 1102	148.80	PDB 84335	748.80

Task 8.4

General ledger

Purchases ledger control

Details	£	Details	£
Purchases returns etc	333.60	Purchases etc	4,148.40
Bank	3,053.37		
Discounts received	35.00		

VAT

Details	£	Details	£
Purchases etc	691.40	Purchases returns etc	55.60
Bank	55.54		

Purchases

Details	£	Details	£
PLCA	2,711.00		
Bank	277.70		

Discounts received

Details	£	Details	£
		PLCA	35.00

Purchases ledger

P J Phillips

Details	£	Details	£
PRDB 04216	117.60	PDB 03576	428.40
CB 002147	806.40	PDB 03598	495.60

Trenter Ltd

Details	£	Details	£
CB 002144	1,105.07	PDB 18435	513.60
CB discount	10.00	PDB 18478	625.20
		PDB 18491	441.60

W J Jones

Details	£	Details	£
PRDB CN0643	67.20	PDB 43654	252.00
CB 002146	252.00	PDB 43681	124.80

O & P Ltd

Details	£	Details	£
PRDB CN1102	148.80	PDB 84335	748.80
CB 002150	580.00		
CB discount	20.00		

Packing Supplies

Details	£	Details	£
CB 002149	309.90	PDB 28423	321.60
CB discount	5.00	PDB 28444	196.80

Task 8.5

(a)

General ledger

Account name	Amount £	Debit ✓	Credit ✓
Petty cash	108.32		✓
VAT	15.52	✓	
Office expenses	15.20	✓	
Stationery	32.60	✓	
Maintenance	45.00	✓	

(b) The credit entry to petty cash would not be needed if the petty cash book was itself part of the general ledger double entry system.

Task 8.6

(a)

Supplier account code	VIN234
General ledger code	GL505

(b) The correct answer is: to help trace relevant accounts quickly and easily

Chapter 9

Task 9.1

Ledger account	Balance	Debit ✓	Credit ✓
Sales	592,513		✓
Telephone	1,295	✓	
Sales ledger control	52,375	✓	
Wages	104,288	✓	
Purchases returns	8,229		✓
Bank overdraft	17,339		✓
Purchases	372,589	✓	
Drawings	71,604	✓	
Sales returns	32,800	✓	
Car	14,700	✓	
Purchases ledger control	31,570		✓

Task 9.2

	£	Debit £	Credit £
Motor vehicles	76,800	76,800	
Office equipment	36,440	36,440	
Sales	285,600		285,600
Purchases	196,800	196,800	
Bank overdraft	2,016		2,016
Petty cash	36	36	
Capital	90,000		90,000
Sales returns	5,640	5,640	
Purchases returns	4,320		4,320
Sales ledger control	42,960	42,960	

	£	Debit £	Credit £
Purchases ledger control	36,120		36,120
VAT owed to HMRC	15,540		15,540
Drawings	12,040	12,040	
Telephone	1,920	1,920	
Electricity	3,360	3,360	
Wages	74,520	74,520	
Loan from bank	36,000		36,000
Discounts allowed	7,680	7,680	
Discounts received	4,680		4,680
Rent expense	16,080	16,080	
Totals		474,276	474,276

Task 9.3

	Debit balances	Credit balances
✓	Assets and expenses	Liabilities, capital and income

Task 9.4

The correct answer is: a liability or income

Task 9.5

The correct answer is: bank overdraft

Task 9.6

	£	Debit £	Credit £
Bank overdraft	4,838		4,838
Capital	216,000		216,000
Discounts allowed	18,432	18,432	
Discounts received	11,232		11,232
Drawings	28,896	28,896	
Electricity	8,064	8,064	
Loan from bank	86,400		86,400
Motor vehicles	184,320	184,320	
Office equipment	87,456	87,456	
Petty cash	100	100	
Purchases	472,320	472,320	
Purchases ledger control	86,688		86,688
Purchases returns	10,368		10,368
Rent expense	38,592	38,592	
Sales	685,440		685,440
Sales ledger control	103,104	103,104	
Sales returns	13,536	13,536	
Telephone	4,608	4,608	
VAT owed to HMRC	37,310		37,310
Wages	178,848	178,848	
Totals		1,138,276	1,138,276

AAT PRACTICE ASSESSMENT 1
BASIC ACCOUNTING I

Time allowed: 2 hours

Basic Accounting I AAT practice assessment 1

All answers should be rounded to the nearest penny unless otherwise instructed.

Section 1

Task 1.1

The following transactions all took place on 30 June and have been entered into the sales day book as shown below. No entries have yet been made into the ledger system.

Sales day book

Date 20XX	Details	Invoice number	Total £	VAT @ 20% £	Net £
30 Jun	West and Webb	1600	9,600	1,600	8,000
30 Jun	Kelly and Co	1601	11,520	1,920	9,600
30 Jun	Bradley Delights	1602	3,936	656	3,280
30 Jun	Burgess Wholesale	1603	7,344	1,224	6,120
	Totals		32,400	5,400	27,000

(a) **What will be the entries in the sales ledger?**

Sales ledger

Account name	Amount £	Debit ✓	Credit ✓
▼			
▼			
▼			
▼			

Picklist:

Bradley Delights
Burgess Wholesale
Kelly and Co
Purchases
Purchases ledger control
Purchases returns
Sales
Sales ledger control
Sales returns
VAT
West and Webb

(b) **What will be the entries in the general ledger?**

General ledger

Account name		Amount £	Debit ✓	Credit ✓
	▼			
	▼			
	▼			

Picklist:

Bradley Delights
Burgess Wholesale
Kelly and Co
Purchases
Purchases ledger control
Purchases returns
Sales
Sales ledger control
Sales returns
VAT
West and Webb

Task 1.2

The following credit transactions all took place on 30 June and have been entered into the purchases returns day book as shown below. No entries have yet been made in the ledgers.

Purchases returns day book

Date 20XX	Details	Credit note number	Total £	VAT @ 20% £	Net £
30 June	Hanover Ltd	1499	2,160	360	1,800
30 June	Lawson Ltd	PO1098	480	80	400
	Totals		2,640	440	2,200

(a) **What will be the entries in the purchases ledger?**

Purchases ledger

Account name		Amount £	Debit ✓	Credit ✓
	▼			
	▼			

Picklist:

Hanover Ltd
Lawson Ltd
Purchases
Purchases ledger control
Purchases returns
Sales
Sales ledger control
Sales returns
VAT

(b) **What will be the entries in the general ledger?**

General ledger

Account name		Amount £	Debit ✓	Credit ✓
	▼			
	▼			
	▼			

Picklist:

Hanover Ltd
Lawson Ltd
Purchases
Purchases ledger control
Purchases returns
Sales
Sales ledger control
Sales returns
VAT

Task 1.3

The following transactions all took place on 30 June and have been entered in the debit side of the cash book as shown below. No entries have yet been made in the ledgers.

Cash book – Debit side

Date 20XX	Details	Discounts £	Bank £
30 Jun	Balance b/d		5,236
30 Jun	RBL Ltd	150	6,000

(a) **What will be the TWO entries in the sales ledger?**

Sales ledger

Account name		Amount £	Debit ✓	Credit ✓
	▼			
	▼			

Picklist:

Balance b/d
Bank
Discounts allowed
Discounts received
Purchases ledger control
RBL Ltd
Sales ledger control

(b) **What will be the THREE entries in the general ledger?**

General ledger

Account name		Amount £	Debit ✓	Credit ✓
	▼			
	▼			
	▼			

Picklist:

Balance b/d
Bank
Discounts allowed
Discounts received
Purchases ledger control
RBL Ltd
Sales ledger control

The following transactions all took place on 30 June and have been entered in the credit side of the cash book as shown below. No entries have yet been made in the ledgers.

Cash book – Credit side

Date 20XX	Details	VAT @ 20% £	Bank £
30 Jun	Office expenses	16	96
30 Jun	Insurance		400

(c) **What will be the entries in the general ledger?**

General ledger

Account name		Amount £	Debit ✓	Credit ✓
	▼			
	▼			
	▼			

Picklist:

Bank
Insurance
Office expenses
Purchases ledger control
Sales ledger control
VAT

....

Task 1.4

Kitchen Kuts maintains a petty cash book as both a book of prime entry and part of the double entry accounting system. The following transactions all took place on 30 June and have been entered in the petty cash book as shown below. No entries have yet been made in the general ledger.

Petty cash book

Date 20XX	Details	Amount £	Date 20XX	Details	Amount £	VAT @ 20% £	Postage £	Motor expenses £	Office expenses £
30 Jun	Balance b/d	118.0	30 Jun	Fuel	19.20	3.20		16.00	
30 Jun	Bank	82.0	30 Jun	Post office	20.00		20.00		
			30 Jun	Motor repair	43.20	7.20		36.00	
			30 Jun	Envelopes	14.40	2.40			12.00
			30 Jun	Balance c/d	103.20				
Totals		200.0			200.00	12.80	20.00	52.00	12.00

What will be the FIVE entries in the general ledger?

General ledger

Account name		Amount £	Debit ✓	Credit ✓
	▼			
	▼			
	▼			
	▼			
	▼			

Picklist:

Balance b/d
Balance c/d
Bank
Envelopes
Fuel
Motor expenses
Motor repair
Office expenses
Petty cash book
Post Office
Postage
VAT

Task 1.5

The following two accounts are in the general ledger at the close of day on 30 June.

(a) **Insert the balance carried down together with date and details.**
(b) **Insert the totals.**
(c) **Insert the balance brought down together with date and details.**

Telephone

Date 20XX	Details	Amount £	Date 20XX	Details	Amount £
01 Jun	Balance b/d	1,320		▼	
26 Jun	Bank	279		▼	
	▼			▼	
	Total			Total	
	▼			▼	

Picklist:

Balance b/d
Balance c/d
Bank
Purchases ledger control

Discounts received

Date 20XX	Details	Amount £	Date 20XX	Details	Amount £
	▼		01 Jun	Balance b/d	1,000
	▼		22 Jun	Purchases ledger control	200
	▼			▼	
	Total			Total	
	▼			▼	

Picklist:

Balance b/d
Balance c/d
Bank
Purchases ledger control

Task 1.6

Below is a list of balances to be transferred to the trial balance as at 30 June.

Write in the figures in the debit or credit column, as appropriate, and total each column.

Account name	Amount £	Debit £	Credit £
Motor vehicles	26,300		
Inventory	19,445		
Bank overdraft	11,463		
Petty cash control	300		
Sales ledger control	169,037		
Purchases ledger control	46,186		
VAT owing to HM Revenue & Customs	26,520		
Capital	17,019		
Loan from bank	16,500		
Sales	438,203		
Sales returns	4,660		
Purchases	264,387		
Purchases returns	674		
Discount received	1,200		
Discount allowed	1,840		
Wages	52,199		
Motor expenses	2,953		
Stationery	2,450		
Rent and rates	8,000		
Advertising	1,349		
Hotel expenses	1,224		
Telephone	1,599		
Subscriptions	360		
Miscellaneous expenses	1,662		
Totals			

Section 2

Task 2.1

Sales invoices have been prepared and partially entered in the sales day book, as shown below.

(a) **Complete the entries in the sales day book by inserting the appropriate figures for each invoice.**

(b) **Total the last five columns of the sales day book.**

Sales day book

Date 20XX	Details	Invoice number	Total £	VAT @ 20% £	Net £	Sales type 1 £	Sales type 2 £
30 Jun	BGS Ltd	3105		3,000		15,000	
30 Jun	S Hopkins	3106	3,120				2,600
30 Jun	Kaur Ltd	3107	480		400	400	
	Totals						

....

Task 2.2

A supply of cardboard boxes has been delivered to Kitchen Kuts by Benson Boards. The purchase order sent from Kitchen Kuts, and the invoice from Benson Boards, are shown below.

Kitchen Kuts
14 High Street
Darton, DF11 4GX

Purchase Order No. KK1067

To: Benson Boards

Date: 7 July 20XX

Please supply 500 cardboard boxes product code 190467
Purchase price: £50 per 100, plus VAT
Discount: less 20% trade discount, as agreed.

Benson Boards
21 High Street, Darton, DF12 5PR
VAT Registration No. 398 3877 00

Invoice No. 3278

Kitchen Kuts
14 High Street
Darton, DF11 4GX

10 July 20XX

500 .... cardboard boxes product code 190467 @ £0.50 each	£250.00
VAT @ 20%	£ 50.00
Total	£300.00

Terms: 30 days net

Check the invoice against the purchase order and answer the following questions.

	Yes ✓	No ✓
Has the correct purchase price of the cardboard boxes been charged?		
Has the correct discount been applied?		
What would be the VAT amount charged if the invoice was correct?	£	
What would be the total amount charged if the invoice was correct?	£	

Task 2.3

Kitchen Kuts codes all purchase invoices with a supplier code AND a general ledger code. A selection of the codes used is given below.

Supplier	Supplier Account Code
ABC Ltd	ABC32
Carlton Products	CAR14
Carter Couriers	CAR20
Farley Fans	FAR11
Johston Ltd	JOH18

Item	General Ledger Code
Kitchen doors	GL107
Kitchen equipment	GL110
Kitchen fans	GL113
Kitchen handles	GL117
Kitchen shelves	GL120

This is an invoice received from a supplier.

Carlton Products **36 Lower Dart Street, Darton, DF13 4PX** **VAT Registration No. 298 3997 00**	
Kitchen Kuts 14 High Street Darton, DF11 4GX	20 July 20XX
80 .... Fancy handles for kitchen doors @ £0.70 each	£56.00
VAT @ 20%	£11.20
Total	£67.20

(a) **Select which codes would be used to code this invoice.**

Supplier account code	▼
General ledger code	▼

Picklist:
ABC32
CAR14
CAR20
FAR11
JOH18
GL107
GL110
GL113
GL117
GL120

(b) **Why is it necessary to use a general ledger code?**

▼

Picklist:
To help when bar coding an item of inventory
To help when filing a financial document
To help trace relevant accounts quickly and easily
To help find the total amount owing to a supplier

Task 2.4

Shown below is a statement of account received from a credit supplier, and the supplier's account as shown in the purchases ledger of Kitchen Kuts.

B Grey Ltd
26 Winfield Road, Darton, DF15 8RL

To: Kitchen Kuts
14 High Street
Darton, DF11 4GX

STATEMENT OF ACCOUNT

Date 20XX	Invoice Number	Details	Invoice Amount £	Cheque Amount £	Balance £
1 April	308	Goods	6,000		6,000
3 May	342	Goods	1,600		7,600
7 May	355	Goods	900		8,500
26 May	368	Goods	1,100		9,600
1 June		Cheque		1,500	8,100

B Grey Ltd

Date 20XX	Details	Amount £	Date 20XX	Details	Amount £
1 June	Bank	1,500	1 April	Purchases	6,000
25 June	Bank	4,000	10 May	Purchases	1,600
			26 May	Purchases	900

(a) **Which item is missing from the statement of account from B Grey Ltd?**

Picklist:

Invoice 308
Invoice 342
Invoice 355
Invoice 368
Cheque for £1,500
Cheque for £4,000

(b) **Which item is missing from the supplier account in Kitchen Kuts' purchases ledger?**

▼

Picklist:

Invoice 308
Invoice 342
Invoice 355
Invoice 368
Cheque for £1,500
Cheque for £4,000

(c) **Assuming any differences between the statement of account from B Grey Ltd and the supplier account in Kitchen Kuts' purchases ledger are simply due to omission errors, what is the amount owing to B Grey Ltd?**

£	

....

Task 2.5

Kitchen Kuts sends out cheques to suppliers on the last day of the month following the month of invoice. Below is an extract from the purchases ledger of Kitchen Kuts.

Paton Payne Ltd

Date 20XX	Details	Amount £	Date 20XX	Details	Amount £
30 June	Bank	4,230	12 May	Balance b/d	4,230
15 June	Purchases returns credit note 126	1,128	10 June	Purchases Invoice 761	4,700
			1 July	Purchases Invoice 812	690

(a) **Complete the remittance advice note below.**

Kitchen Kuts
14 High Street
Darton, DF11 4GX

REMITTANCE ADVICE

To: Paton Payne Ltd   Date: 31 July 20XX

Please find attached our cheque in payment of the following amounts.

Invoice number	Credit note number	Amount £
	Total amount paid	

(b) **Which of the following statements is true?**

	✓
The remittance advice note will be sent to the customer to advise them of the amount being paid	
The remittance advice note will be sent to the supplier's bank to advise them of the amount being paid	
The remittance advice note will be sent to the supplier to advise them of the amount being paid	
The remittance advice note will be sent to the accounts department at Paton Payne Ltd to request that a cheque is raised	

Task 2.6

On 1 July Kitchen Kuts delivered the following goods to a credit customer, Churchill Stores.

Kitchen Kuts
14 High Street, Darton, DF11 4GX.

Delivery note No. 21765
01 July 20XX

Churchill Stores   Customer account code: CH152
20 The Mall
New Meldon
Surrey, SR11 5BS

100 cases of product code F100.

The list price of the goods was £5 per case plus VAT. Churchill Stores are to be given a 20% trade discount and a 2% early settlement discount.

(a) **Complete the invoice below.**

Kitchen Kuts
14 High Street, Darton, DF11 4GX.

VAT Registration No. 298 3827 04

Churchill Stores   Customer account code:
20 The Mall
New Meldon   Delivery note number:
Surrey, SR11 5BS

                                                            Date: 1 July 20XX

Invoice No: 298

Quantity of cases	Product code	Total list price £	Net amount after discount £	VAT £	Gross £

Kitchen Kuts offers each customer a discount of 10% if any order amounts to £5,000 or over.

(b) **What is the name of this type of discount?**

▼

Picklist:

Bulk discount
Settlement discount
Trade discount

Task 2.7

The following is a summary of transactions with Etties Ltd, a new credit customer.

£3,525 re invoice 3070 of 12 July
£1,175 re invoice 3120 of 20 July
£752 re credit note 103 of 21 July
£846 re invoice 3134 of 27 July
Cheque for £1,800 received 29 July

Complete the statement of account below.

Kitchen Kuts Ltd
14 High Street
Darton
DF11 4GX

To: Etties Ltd
Date: 31 July 20XX

Date 20XX	Details	Transaction amount £	Outstanding amount £
12 July	Invoice 3070		
20 July	Invoice 3120		
21 July	Credit note 103		
27 July	Invoice 3134		
29 July	Cheque		

- -

Task 2.8

The account shown below is in the sales ledger of Kitchen Kuts. A cheque for £1,927 has now been received from this customer.

L Fortnum Ltd

Date 20XX	Details	Amount £	Date 20XX	Details	Amount £
1 May	Balance b/d	3,525	2 June	Bank	3,525
20 May	Sales invoice 398	1,180	26 June	Sales returns credit note 110	1,128
30 June	Sales Invoice 401	3,055			

(a) **Which item has not been included in the payment?**

Picklist:

Balance b/d
Sales invoice 398
Sales invoice 401
Bank
Sales returns credit note 110

An invoice is being prepared to be sent to L Fortnum Ltd for £1,080.00 plus VAT of £205.20. A settlement discount of 5% will be offered for payment within 10 days.

(b) **What is the amount Kitchen Kuts should receive if payment is made within 10 days?**

£ [   ]

(c) **What is the amount Kitchen Kuts should receive if payment is NOT made within 10 days?**

£ [   ]

Task 2.9

It is important to understand the difference between capital expenditure, revenue, expenditure, capital income and revenue income.

Select one option in each instance below to show whether the item will be capital expenditure, revenue expenditure, capital income or revenue income.

Item	Capital expenditure ✓	Revenue expenditure ✓	Capital income ✓	Revenue income ✓
Receipts from sales of goods to credit customers				
Receipts from cash sales				
Receipt from sale of Kitchen Kuts' delivery van				
Purchase of motor vehicle				
Purchase of goods for resale				
Purchase of stationery using petty cash				

Task 2.10

Financial accounting is based upon the accounting equation.

(a) **Show whether the following statements are True or False.**

	True ✓	False ✓
Assets less liabilities are equal to capital		
Capital plus assets are equal to liabilities		
Capital less liabilities are equal to assets		

(b) **Classify each of the following items as an asset or a liability.**

Item	Asset or liability?
Motor van	
Bank loan	
Money owing from trade receivables	

AAT PRACTICE ASSESSMENT 1
BASIC ACCOUNTING I

ANSWERS

Basic Accounting I AAT practice assessment 1

Section 1

Task 1.1

(a)

Sales ledger

Account name	Amount £	Debit ✓	Credit ✓
West and Webb	9,600	✓	
Kelly and Co	11,520	✓	
Bradley Delights	3,936	✓	
Burgess Wholesale	7,344	✓	

(b)

General ledger

Account name	Amount £	Debit ✓	Credit ✓
Sales	27,000		✓
VAT	5,400		✓
Sales ledger control	32,400	✓	

Task 1.2

(a)

Purchases ledger

Account name	Amount £	Debit ✓	Credit ✓
Hanover Ltd	2,160	✓	
Lawson Ltd	480	✓	

(b)

General ledger

Account name	Amount £	Debit ✓	Credit ✓
Purchases ledger control	2,640	✓	
Purchases returns	2,200		✓
VAT	440		✓

Task 1.3

(a)

Sales ledger

Account name	Amount £	Debit ✓	Credit ✓
RBL Ltd	6,000		✓
RBL Ltd	150		✓

(b)

General ledger

Account name	Amount £	Debit ✓	Credit ✓
Discounts allowed	150	✓	
Sales ledger control	6,000		✓
Sales ledger control	150		✓

(c)

General ledger

Account name	Amount £	Debit ✓	Credit ✓
Office expenses	80	✓	
VAT	16	✓	
Insurance	400	✓	

Task 1.4

General ledger

Account name	Amount £	Debit ✓	Credit ✓
VAT	12.80	✓	
Postage	20.00	✓	
Motor expenses	52.00	✓	
Office expenses	12.00	✓	
Bank	82.00		✓

Task 1.5

Telephone

Date 20XX	Details	Amount £	Date 20XX	Details £	Amount £
01 Jun	Balance b/d	1,320			
26 Jun	Bank	279			
			30 Jun	Balance c/d	1,599
	Total	1,599		Total	1,599
1 Jul	Balance b/d	1,599			

Discounts received

Date 20XX	Details	Amount £	Date 20XX	Details £	Amount £
			01 Jun	Balance b/d	1,000
			22 Jun	Purchases ledger control	200
30 Jun	Balance c/d	1,200			
	Total	1,200		Total	1,200
			1 Jul	Balance b/d	1,200

Task 1.6

Account name	Amount £	Debit £	Credit £
Motor vehicles	26,300	26,300	
Inventory	19,445	19,445	
Bank overdraft	11,463		11,463
Petty cash control	300	300	
Sales ledger control	169,037	169,037	
Purchases ledger control	46,186		46,186
VAT owing to HM Revenue & Customs	26,520		26,520
Capital	17,019		17,019
Loan from bank	16,500		16,500
Sales	438,203		438,203
Sales returns	4,660	4,660	
Purchases	264,387	264,387	
Purchases returns	674		674
Discount received	1,200		1,200
Discount allowed	1,840	1,840	
Wages	52,199	52,199	
Motor expenses	2,953	2,953	
Stationery	2,450	2,450	
Rent and rates	8,000	8,000	
Advertising	1,349	1,349	
Hotel expenses	1,224	1,224	
Telephone	1,599	1,599	
Subscriptions	360	360	
Miscellaneous expenses	1,662	1,662	
Totals		557,765	557,765

Section 2

Task 2.1

Sales day book

Date 20XX	Details	Invoice number	Total £	VAT £	Net £	Sales type 1 £	Sales type 2 £
30 Jun	BGS Ltd	3105	18,000	3,000	15,000	15,000	
30 Jun	S Hopkins	3106	3,120	520	2,600		2,600
30 Jun	Kaur Ltd	3107	480	80	400	400	
	Totals		21,600	3,600	18,000	15,400	2,600

Task 2.2

	Yes ✓	No ✓
Has the correct purchase price of the cardboard boxes been charged?	✓	
Has the correct discount been applied?		✓
What would be the VAT amount charged if the invoice was correct?	£	40
What would be the total amount charged if the invoice was correct?	£	240

Task 2.3

(a)

Supplier account code	CAR14
General ledger code	GL117

(b) The correct answer is: to help trace relevant accounts quickly and easily

Task 2.4

(a) The correct answer is: cheque for £4,000

(b) The correct answer is: invoice 368

(c) The correct answer is: £4,100 (8,100 – 4,000 = 4,100)

Task 2.5

(a)

	Kitchen Kuts 14 High Street Darton, DF11 4GX **REMITTANCE ADVICE**	
To: Paton Payne Ltd		Date: 31 July 20XX
Please find attached our cheque in payment of the following amounts.		

Invoice number	Credit note number	Amount £
761		4,700
	126	1,128
	Total amount paid	3,572

(b) The correct answer is: the remittance advice note will be sent to the supplier to advise them of the amount being paid

Task 2.6

(a) VAT: (400 – (400 × 2/100)) × 20/100 = £78.40

Kitchen Kuts
14 High Street, Darton, DF11 4GX.

VAT Registration No. 298 3827 04

Churchill Stores
CH152
20 The Mall
New Meldon
21765
Surrey, SR11 5BS

Customer account code:

Delivery note number:

Date: 1 July 20XX

Invoice No: 298

Quantity of cases	Product code	Total list price £	Net amount after discount £	VAT £	Gross £
100	F100	500.00	400.00	78.40	478.40

(b)   The correct answer is: bulk discount

Task 2.7

Kitchen Kuts Ltd
14 High Street
Darton
DF11 4GX

To: Etties Ltd

Date: 31 July 20XX

Date 20XX	Details	Transaction amount £	Outstanding amount £
12 July	Invoice 3070	3,525	3,525
20 July	Invoice 3120	1,175	4,700
21 July	Credit note 103	752	3,948
27 July	Invoice 3134	846	4,794
29 July	Cheque	1,800	2,994

Task 2.8

(a) The correct answer is: Sales invoice 398

(b) The correct answer is: £1,231.20

Working

(£1,080.00 × 95%) + £205.20 = £1,231.20

(c) The correct answer is: £1,285.20

Working

£1,080.00 + £205.20 = £1,285.20

Task 2.9

Item	Capital expenditure ✓	Revenue expenditure ✓	Capital income ✓	Revenue income ✓
Receipts from sales of goods to credit customers				✓
Receipts from cash sales				✓
Receipt from sale of Kitchen Kuts' delivery van			✓	
Purchase of motor vehicle	✓			
Purchase of goods for resale		✓		
Purchase of stationery using petty cash		✓		

Task 2.10

(a)

	True ✓	False ✓
Assets less liabilities are equal to capital	✓	
Capital plus assets are equal to liabilities		✓
Capital less liabilities are equal to assets		✓

(b)

Item	Asset or liability?
Motor van	Asset
Bank loan	Liability
Money owing from trade receivables	Asset

Basic Accounting I AAT practice assessment 2

All answers should be rounded to the nearest penny unless otherwise instructed.

Section 1

Task 1.1

The following transactions all took place on 30 June and have been entered into the sales day book as shown. No entries have yet been made into the ledgers.

Sales day book

Date 20XX	Details	Invoice Number	Total £	VAT £	Net £
30 Jun	L Cohen	1096	864	144	720
30 Jun	JRP Ltd	1097	1,920	320	1,600
30 Jun	Three Bees Ltd	1098	816	136	680
30 Jun	Bradley Brothers	1099	2,400	400	2,000
	Totals		6,000	1,000	5,000

(a) **What will be the entries in the sales ledger?**

Sales ledger

Account name	Amount £	Debit ✓	Credit ✓
▼			
▼			
▼			
▼			

(b) **What will be the entries in the general ledger?**

General ledger

Account name	Amount £	Debit ✓	Credit ✓
▼			
▼			
▼			

Picklist:

Bradley Brothers
JRP Ltd
L Cohen
Purchases
Purchases ledger control
Purchases returns
Sales
Sales ledger control
Sales returns
Three Bees Ltd
VAT

Task 1.2

The following credit transactions all took place on 30 June and have been entered into the purchases returns day book as shown below. No entries have yet been made into the ledgers.

Purchases returns day book

Date 20XX	Details	Credit Note Number	Total £	VAT £	Net £
30 Jun	Bansal Traders	315/1	384	64	320
30 Jun	Rippon Ltd	166	912	152	760
	Totals		1,296	216	1,080

(a) **What will be the entries in the purchases ledger?**

Purchases ledger

Account name	Amount £	Debit ✓	Credit ✓
▼			
▼			

(b) **What will be the entries in the general ledger?**

General ledger

Account name	Amount £	Debit ✓	Credit ✓
▼			
▼			
▼			

Picklist:

Bansal Traders
Purchases
Purchases ledger control
Purchases returns
Rippon Ltd
Sales
Sales ledger control
Sales returns
VAT

Task 1.3

The following transactions all took place on 30 June and have been entered into the cash book as shown below. No entries have yet been made into the ledgers.

Cash book

Date 20XX	Details	Bank £	Date 20XX	Details	VAT £	Bank £
30 Jun	Balance b/d	6,120	30 Jun	Jewan James (trade payable)		3,125
30 Jun	URV Ltd (trade receivable)	1,221	30 Jun	Offices expenses	32	192
			30 Jun	Rent		600

(a) **What will be the entry in the sales ledger?**

Sales ledger

Account name	Amount £	Debit ✓	Credit ✓
▼			

(b)   **What will be the entry in the purchases ledger?**

Purchases ledger

Account name	Amount £	Debit ✓	Credit ✓
▼			

(c)   **What will be the FIVE entries in the general ledger?**

General ledger

Account name	Amount £	Debit ✓	Credit ✓
▼			
▼			
▼			
▼			
▼			

Picklist:

Balance b/d
Jewan James
Office expenses
Purchases
Purchases ledger control
Rent
Sales
Sales ledger control
URV Ltd
VAT

Task 1.4

Gold Ltd maintains a petty cash book as a book of prime entry; it is not part of the double entry accounting system. The following transactions all took place on 30 June and have been entered into the petty cash book as shown below. No entries have yet been made into the general ledger.

Petty cash book

Date 20XX	Details	Amount £	Date 20XX	Details	Amount £	VAT £	Office expenses £	Premises expenses £	Other operating costs £
30 Jun	Opening balance	125.00	30 Jun	Postage stamps	20.00		20.00		
			30 Jun	Plumbing repair	33.60	5.60		28.00	
			30 Jun	Coffee	10.85				10.85
			30 Jun	Closing balance	60.55				
		125.00			125.00	5.60	20.00	28.00	10.85

What will be the FIVE entries in the general ledger, to the nearest penny?

General ledger

Account name	Amount £	Debit ✓	Credit ✓
▼			
▼			
▼			
▼			
▼			

Picklist:

Bank
Closing balance
Coffee
Office expenses
Opening balance
Other operating costs
Petty cash control
Petty cash book
Plumbing repair
Postage stamps
Premises expenses
VAT

Task 1.5

The following two accounts are in the general ledger at the close of day on 30 June.

(a) **Insert the balance carried down together with date and details.**

(b) **Insert the totals.**

(c) **Insert the balance brought down together with date and details.**

Drawings by owner

Date 20XX	Details	Amount £	Date 20XX	Details	Amount £
1 Jun	Balance b/d	12,165		▼	
20 Jun	Cash	250		▼	
	Total			Total	
	▼			▼	

Cash sales

Date 20XX	Details	Amount £	Date 20XX	Details	Amount £
18 Jun	Cash	100	1 Jun	Balance b/d	1,385
	▼		25 Jun	Cash	52
	Total			Total	
	▼			▼	

Picklist:

Balance b/d
Balance c/d
Bank
Cash
Cash sales

Task 1.6

Below is a list of balances to be transferred to the trial balance as at 30 June.

Place the figures in the debit or credit column, as appropriate, and total each column. Do not enter figures with decimal places in this task.

Account name	Amount £	Debit £	Credit £
Sales ledger control	59,216		
Cash at bank	1,980		
Hotel expenses	625		
Purchases ledger control	80,165		
VAT owing from HM Revenue and Customs	825		
Bank interest received	128		
Miscellaneous expenses	1,709		
Premises expenses	2,001		
Motor insurance	2,115		
Capital	27,593		
Motor vehicles	46,422		
Sales returns	305		
Purchases returns	1,499		
Wages	29,615		
Purchases	97,232		
Office equipment	39,397		
Office expenses	5,385		
Commission received	3,000		
Rent and rates	9,855		
Loan from bank	22,500		
Bank charges	245		
Petty cash	250		
Motor expenses	1,588		
Sales	163,880		
Totals			

Section 2

Task 2.1

Purchases credit notes have been received and partially entered in the purchases returns day book, as shown below.

(a) **Complete the entries in the purchases returns day book by inserting the appropriate figures for each credit note.**

Purchases returns day book

Date 20XX	Details	Credit note number	Total £	VAT £	Net £	Purchases type A £	Purchases type B £
30 Jun	Grant Products	3211	1,920				1,600
30 Jun	Dhillon Designs	347		440		2,200	
30 Jun	PPT Ltd	R648			680	680	
30 Jun	O'Connell Ltd	4490			2,000		2,000

(b) **Show whether the following statements are True or False.**

Statements	True ✓	False ✓
Sales day books never include analysis columns.		
Sales credit notes are entered in the sales day book.		

Task 2.2

On 10 July, Gold Ltd returned 50 faulty items to Truman Traders. The original invoice is shown below together with the credit note, which has been stamped by Gold Ltd ready for the relevant checks to be made.

Carry out the checks required and complete the stamped area of the credit note.

Invoice

Truman Traders	
115 Rounds Street	
Darton, DF12 7TP	
VAT Registration No. 325 3165 00	

	Invoice number: 105690
To: Gold Ltd	Date: 10 July 20XX
14 High Street	
Darton DF11 4GX	

	£
60 boxes × 10 ... product 'Hardy' @ £40 per box	2,400.00
Trade discount 15%	360.00
Net price	2,040.00
VAT @ 20%	408.00
Total	2,448.00

Credit note

Truman Traders	
115 Round Street	
Darton, DF12 7TP	
VAT Registration No. 325 3165 00	

To: Gold Ltd	Credit note number: JJ4140
14 High Street	Date: 18 July 20XX
Darton DF11 4GX	

	£
50 ... product 'Hardy' @ £4 each	200.00
VAT @ 20%	40.00
Total	240.00

Stamp, to be completed to the nearest penny		
Has the correct trade discount been applied?		▼
Has the correct settlement discount been applied?		▼
Can this credit note be authorised?		▼
If there is an error, what should be the total amount of the credit note, including VAT?	£	

Picklist:
Yes
No
Not applicable

Task 2.3

Gold Ltd codes all purchases invoices with a supplier account code when they are received. The supplier account codes are made up of the first five letters of the supplier's name, followed by the number of the ledger page allocated to each supplier in that alphabetical group, as shown in the extract below.

Supplier	Supplier account code
Babbannger Ltd	BABBA01
Baltemore Ltd	BALTE02
Brigham Ltd	BRIGH03

On 10 July, an invoice was received from a new supplier, Healy Ltd. There are no suppliers beginning with the letter H. On 14 July, an invoice was received from another new supplier, Hamnet Ltd.

(a) **What will be the account code for Healy Ltd?**

(b) **What will be the account code for Hamnet Ltd?**

(c) **What is the purpose of allocating account codes to suppliers?**

	✓
To ensure accounts can be found quickly and easily in the sales ledger.	
To ensure accounts can be found quickly and easily in the purchases ledger.	
To ensure accounts can be found quickly and easily in the general ledger.	
To comply with legislation.	

Task 2.4

When a statement is received from a supplier it is reconciled with the supplier's account in the purchases ledger. Shown below is a statement of account which has been received from L C Grove and the account of L C Grove in the purchases ledger of Gold Ltd.

L C Grove

135 Farringdon Road, Darton, DF12 3CF

To: Gold Ltd
14 High Street
Darton DF11 4GX

29 May 20XX

STATEMENT OF ACCOUNT

Date 20XX	Invoice/Credit note number	Details	Invoice Amount £	Credit note amount £	Balance £
31 Mar	3982	Goods	1,821		1,821
11 Apr	4012	Goods	298		2,119
17 Apr	4052	Goods	3,426		5,545
01 May	127	Credit note		2,000	3,545
12 May	4261	Goods	1,289		4,834
22 May	4295	Goods	871		5,705

L C Grove

Date 20XX	Details	Amount £	Date 20XX	Details	Amount £
1 May	Purchases returns – CN127	2,000	1 Apr	Balance b/d	1,821
			11 Apr	Purchases – Invoice 4012	298
			12 May	Purchases – Invoice 4261	1,289
			22 May	Purchases – Invoice 4295	871

Complete the reconciliation statement below.

Purchases ledger account reconciliation

L C Grove

Balance outstanding as per supplier statement at 29 May	£ 5,705
▼	£
Balance as per purchases ledger account	£

Picklist:

Invoice 3982 missing from purchases ledger account
Invoice 4012 missing from purchases ledger account
Invoice 4052 missing from purchases ledger account
Invoice 4261 missing from supplier statement
Invoice 4295 missing from supplier statement
Credit note 127 missing from purchases ledger account

Task 2.5

Gold Ltd sends BACS remittance advice notes to suppliers on the last day of the month following the month of invoice. Gold Ltd banks with Midway Bank plc and Grant Metals banks with City4 Bank plc. Below is an extract from the purchases ledger of Gold Ltd.

Grant Metals

Date 20XX	Details	Amount £	Date 20XX	Details	Amount £
10 May	Purchases returns credit note CN298	149	8 May	Purchases invoice 3222	4,260
19 May	Purchases returns credit note CN306	387	20 Jun	Purchases invoice 3250	501
30 Jun	Bank	3,724	1 Jul	Purchases invoice 3301	3,176
			10 Jul	Purchases invoice 3337	1,433

Complete the remittance advice note below.

Gold Ltd
14 High Street
Darton, DF11 4GX

BACS REMITTANCE ADVICE

To: [▼]   Date: [▼]

The following payment will reach your bank account within three working days.

Transaction date	Invoice number	Credit note number	Amount £
[▼]	[▼]	[▼]	[▼]

Picklist under 'To' heading:

City4 Bank plc
Gold Ltd
Grant Metals
Midway Bank plc

Picklist under 'Date' heading:

31 May 20XX
30 June 20XX
31 July 20XX

Picklist under 'Transaction date' heading:

8 May
10 May
19 May
20 June
30 June
1 July
10 July

Picklist under 'Invoice number' heading:

3222
3250
3301
3337
Not applicable

Picklist under 'Credit note number' heading:

CN298
CN306
Not applicable

Task 2.6

On 9 July, Gold Ltd received the following purchase orders from two credit customers. The goods were delivered the following day.

Bradshaw Ltd
300 The Parade
Darton, DF11 9GT

PURCHASE ORDER NO BR121

Gold Ltd   8 July 20XX
14 High Street
Darton
DF11 4GX

Please supply 1,100 units of product code GG160 @ £200.00 per hundred, plus VAT

Trade discount: 15%

SJP Ltd
250 The Avenue
Darton, DF10 9BS

PURCHASE ORDER NO 164S

Gold Ltd   8 July 20XX
14 High Street
Darton
DF11 4GX

Please supply 100 units of product code GG260 @ £9.00 each, plus VAT

Settlement discount for payment within 10 days: 2%

(a)   **Complete the invoices below, to the nearest penny.**

INVOICE NO G1700

Gold Ltd
14 High Street, Darton, DF11 4GX.
VAT Registration No. 298 3827 04

To: Bradshaw Ltd   Date: 10 July 20XX
      300 The Parade
      Darton, DF11 9GT   Purchase order No: BR121

Quantity of units	Product code	Amount before VAT £	VAT £	Gross £
1,100				

INVOICE NO G1701

Gold Ltd
14 High Street, Darton, DF11 4GX.
VAT Registration No. 298 3827 04

To: SJP Ltd
250 The Avenue
Darton, DF10 9BS

Date: 10 July 20XX

Purchase Order No: 164S

Quantity of units	Product code	Amount before VAT £	VAT £	Gross £
100				

Gold Ltd sometimes offers a discount if an order is placed for a large quantity of goods.

(b) **What is the name of this type of discount?**

Picklist:

Account discount
Bulk discount
Commission discount
Trade receivable discount
Early discount

- -

Task 2.7

The following is a summary of transactions with Osborne and Wright, a credit customer.

Opening balance of £2,125
£1,100 re invoice 281 of 6 July
£1,526 re credit note CN61 of 8 July
£3,490 re invoice 283 of 15 July
£1,550 re invoice 287 of 18 July
£726 re invoice 295 of 20 July
£350 re credit note CN68 of 29 July
£1,135 re invoice 300 of 31 July
£420 re credit note CN72 of 31 July

Complete the statement of account below.

STATEMENT OF ACCOUNT

Gold Ltd
14 High Street, Darton, DF11 4GX.

To: Osborne and Wright   Date: 31 July 20XX

Date 20XX	Details	Transaction amount £
1 July	Opening balance	
6 July	Invoice 281	
8 July	Credit note CN61	
15 July	Invoice 283	
18 July	Invoice 287	
20 July	Invoice 295	
29 July	Credit note CN68	
31 July	Invoice 300	
31 July	Credit note CN72	
	Total amount outstanding	

Task 2.8

This is an extract from a sales invoice in Gold Ltd's sales ledger

Invoice number: 1505	
Date: 10 July 20XX	
Terms: 6% settlement discount for payment within 7 days.	
Net amount	£1,000.00
VAT	£188.00

A cheque for £1,128.00 was received on 16 July 20XX

(a) **Has the correct amount been paid?**

	✓
Yes, the cheque was received too late to claim the discount	
Yes, the cheque was received within 7 days and the discount was taken	
No, the cheque was received too late to claim the discount.	
No, the cheque was received within 7 days and the discount was not taken.	

This is a list of transactions in an account in Gold Ltd's sales ledger.

	£
Invoice 101	470
Invoice 109	2,244
Credit note 26	758
Invoice 126	220
Cheque	695
Invoice 141	2,450
Invoice 150	1,288
Credit note 40	500

A cheque has been received for £4,999.

(b) **What TWO items have not been included in the payment?**

	✓
Invoice 101	
Invoice 109	
Credit note 26	
Invoice 126	
Cheque	
Invoice 141	
Invoice 150	
Credit note 40	

Task 2.9

It is important to understand the difference between capital expenditure, revenue expenditure, capital income and revenue income.

Select one option in each instance below to complete the sentence.

1 Capital income occurs when | ▼ |

2 Revenue income occurs when | ▼ |

3 Capital expenditure occurs when | ▼ |

4 Revenue expenditure occurs when | ▼ |

5 A receipt in relation to a VAT refund is classed as | ▼ |

6 The purchase of postage stamps from petty cash is classed as | ▼ |

Picklist for questions 1 to 4:

A purchase, alteration or improvement of an asset takes place
A purchase is made relating to day to day running expenses
Revenue exceeds expenditure
Money is received relating to one-off transactions such as the sale of an asset
Money is received relating to regular transactions such as sales
The capital account is overdrawn
The drawings account has a credit balance

Picklist for questions 5 and 6:

Capital expenditure
Capital income
Revenue expenditure
Revenue income

Task 2.10

Financial accounting is based upon the accounting equation.

(a) Show whether the following statements are True or False.

Statements	True ✓	False ✓
Liabilities less capital are equal to assets.		
Capital plus liabilities are equal to assets.		
Assets less liabilities are equal to capital.		

(b) **Insert the correct answer to each of the following questions.**

Question	Answer £
If assets total £10,000 and liabilities total £5,000 what is the amount of capital?	
If capital totals £36,000 and assets total £45,000 what is the amount of liabilities?	
If liabilities total £15,000 and capital totals £68,000 what is the amount of assets?	

AAT PRACTICE ASSESSMENT 2
BASIC ACCOUNTING I

ANSWERS

Basic Accounting I AAT practice assessment 2

Section 1

Task 1.1

(a)

Sales ledger

Account name	Amount £	Debit	Credit
L Cohen	864	✓	
JRP Ltd	1,920	✓	
Three Bees Ltd	816	✓	
Bradley Brothers	2,400	✓	

(b)

General ledger

Account name	Amount £	Debit	Credit
Sales ledger control	6,000	✓	
Sales	5,000		✓
VAT	1,000		✓

Task 1.2

(a)

Purchases ledger

Account name	Amount £	Debit	Credit
Bansal Traders	384	✓	
Rippon Ltd	912	✓	

(b)

General ledger

Account name	Amount £	Debit	Credit
Purchases ledger control	1,296	✓	
Purchases returns	1,080		✓
VAT	216		✓

Task 1.3

(a)

Sales ledger

Account name	Amount £	Debit	Credit
URV Ltd	1,221		✓

(b)

Purchases ledger

Account name	Amount £	Debit	Credit
Jewan James	3,125	✓	

(c)

General ledger

Account name	Amount £	Debit	Credit
Purchases ledger control	3,125	✓	
Office expenses	160	✓	
VAT	32	✓	
Rent	600	✓	
Sales ledger control	1,221		✓

Task 1.4

General ledger

Account name	Amount £	Debit	Credit
VAT	5.60	✓	
Office expenses	20.00	✓	
Premises expenses	28.00	✓	
Other operating costs	10.85	✓	
Petty cash control	64.45		✓

Task 1.5

Drawings by owner

Date 20XX	Details	Amount £	Date 20XX	Details	Amount £
1 Jun	Balance b/d	12,165	30 Jun	Balance c/d	12,415
20 Jun	Cash	250			
	Total	12,415		Total	12,415
1 Jul	Balance b/d	12,415			

Cash sales

Date 20XX	Details	Amount £	Date 20XX	Details	Amount £
18 Jun	Cash	100	1 Jun	Balance b/d	1,385
30 Jun	Balance c/d	1,337	25 Jun	Cash	52
	Total	1,437		Total	1,437
			1 Jul	Balance b/d	1,337

Task 1.6

Account name	Amount £	Debit £	Credit £
Sales ledger control	59,216	59,216	
Cash at bank	1,980	1,980	
Hotel expenses	625	625	
Purchases ledger control	80,165		80,165
VAT owing from HM Revenue and Customs	825	825	
Bank interest received	128		128
Miscellaneous expenses	1,709	1,709	
Premises expenses	2,001	2,001	
Motor insurance	2,115	2,115	
Capital	27,593		27,593
Motor vehicles	46,422	46,422	
Sales returns	305	305	
Purchases returns	1,499		1,499
Wages	29,615	29,615	
Purchases	97,232	97,232	
Office equipment	39,397	39,397	
Office expenses	5,385	5,385	
Commission received	3,000		3,000
Rent and rates	9,855	9,855	
Loan from bank	22,500		22,500
Bank charges	245	245	
Petty cash	250	250	
Motor expenses	1,588	1,588	
Sales	163,880		163,880
Totals		298,765	298,765

Section 2

Task 2.1

(a)

Purchases returns day book

Date 20XX	Details	Credit note number	Total £	VAT £	Net £	Purchases type A £	Purchases type B £
30 Jun	Grant Products	3211	1,920	320	1,600		1,600
30 Jun	Dhillon Designs	347	2,640	440	2,200	2,200	
30 Jun	PPT Ltd	R648	816	136	680	680	
30 Jun	O'Connell Ltd	4490	2,400	400	2,000		2,000

(b)

Statements	True	False
Sales day books never include analysis columns.		✓
Sales credit notes are entered in the sales day book.		✓

Task 2.2

VAT: £200 − (£200 × 15/100) × 1.2 = £204.00

Has the correct trade discount been applied?	No
Has the correct settlement discount been applied?	Not applicable
Can this credit note be authorised?	No
If there is an error, what should be the total amount of the credit note, including VAT?	£ 204.00

Task 2.3

(a)

HEALY01

(b)

HAMNE02

(c) The correct answer is: to ensure accounts can be found quickly and easily in the purchases ledger.

Task 2.4

Purchases ledger account reconciliation
L C Grove

	£	
Balance outstanding as per supplier statement at 29 May	£	5,705
Invoice 4052 missing from purchases ledger account	£	3,426
Balance as per purchases ledger account	£	2,279

Task 2.5

<table>
<tr><td colspan="4" align="center">Gold Ltd
14 High Street
Darton, DF11 4GX

BACS REMITTANCE ADVICE</td></tr>
<tr><td colspan="2">To: Grant Metals</td><td colspan="2">Date: 31 July 20XX</td></tr>
<tr><td colspan="4">The following payment will reach your bank account within three working days.</td></tr>
<tr><td>Transaction date</td><td>Invoice number</td><td>Credit note number</td><td>Amount
£</td></tr>
<tr><td>20 June</td><td>3250</td><td>Not applicable</td><td>501</td></tr>
</table>

Task 2.6

(a)

<table>
<tr><td colspan="5" align="center">INVOICE NO G1700

Gold Ltd
14 High Street, Darton, DF11 4GX.
VAT Registration No. 298 3827 04</td></tr>
<tr><td colspan="3">To: Bradshaw Ltd
       300 The Parade
       Darton, DF11 9GT</td><td colspan="2">Date: 10 July 20XX

Purchase order No: BR121</td></tr>
<tr><td>Quantity of units</td><td>Product code</td><td>Amount before VAT
£</td><td>VAT
£</td><td>Gross
£</td></tr>
<tr><td>1,100</td><td>GG160</td><td>1,870</td><td>374</td><td>2,244</td></tr>
</table>

INVOICE NO G1701

Gold Ltd
14 High Street, Darton, DF11 4GX.
VAT Registration No. 298 3827 04

To: SJP Ltd
250 The Avenue
Darton, DF10 9BS

Date: 10 July 20XX

Purchase Order No: 164S

Quantity of units	Product code	Amount before VAT £	VAT £	Gross £
100	GG260	900	176.40	1,076.40

(b)

Bulk discount

Task 2.7

STATEMENT OF ACCOUNT

Gold Ltd
14 High Street, Darton, DF11 4GX.

To: Osborne and Wright   Date: 31 July 20XX

Date 20XX	Details	Transaction amount £
1 July	Opening balance	2,125
6 July	Invoice 281	1,100
8 July	Credit note CN61	1,526
15 July	Invoice 283	3,490
18 July	Invoice 287	1,550
20 July	Invoice 295	726
29 July	Credit note CN68	350
31 July	Invoice 300	1,135
31 July	Credit note CN72	420
	Total amount outstanding	7,830

Task 2.8

(a)   The correct answer is: yes, the cheque was received within 7 days and the discount was taken.

(b)   The correct answer is: invoice 126 and credit note 40 were not included.

Workings

	£
Invoice 101	470
Invoice 109	2,244
Credit note 26	(758)
Invoice 126	220
Cheque	(695)
Invoice 141	2,450
Invoice 150	1,288
Credit note 40	(500)
Total	4,719
Amount of cheque	4,999
Difference	(280)
Invoice 126	220
Credit note 40	(500)
Difference	(280)

Task 2.9

The correct answers are:

1   Capital income occurs when money is received relating to one-off transactions such as the sale of an asset.

2   Revenue income occurs when money is received relating to regular transactions such as sales.

3   Capital expenditure occurs when a purchase, alteration or improvement of an asset takes place.

4   Revenue expenditure occurs when a purchase is made relating to day-to-day running expenses.

5   A receipt in relation to a VAT refund is classed as revenue income.

6   The purchase of postage stamps from petty cash is classed as revenue expenditure.

Task 2.10

(a)

Statements	True ✓	False ✓
Liabilities less capital are equal to assets.		✓
Capital plus liabilities are equal to assets.	✓	
Assets less liabilities are equal to capital.	✓	

(b)

Question	Answer £
If assets total £10,000 and liabilities total £5,000 what is the amount of capital?	5,000
If capital totals £36,000 and assets total £45,000 what is the amount of liabilities?	9,000
If liabilities total £15,000 and capital totals £68,000 what is the amount of assets?	83,000

AAT PRACTICE ASSESSMENT 3
BASIC ACCOUNTING I

Time allowed: 2 hours

Basic Accounting I AAT practice assessment 3

All answers should be rounded to the nearest penny unless otherwise instructed.

Section 1

Task 1.1

The following transactions all took place on 30 June and have been entered into the sales day book as shown below. No entries have yet been made into the ledgers.

Sales day book

Date 20XX	Details	Invoice number	Total £	VAT £	Net £
30 Jun	BGH Ltd	3745	4,320	720	3,600
30 Jun	Stockley & Co	3746	1,296	216	1,080
30 Jun	RL Turner	3747	2,544	424	2,120
30 Jun	Knowle plc	3748	1,008	168	840
	Totals		9,168	1,528	7,640

(a) **What will be the entries in the sales ledger?**

Sales ledger

Account name	Amount £	Debit ✓	Credit ✓
▼			
▼			
▼			
▼			

(b) **What will be the entries in the general ledger?**

General ledger

Account name	Amount £	Debit ✓	Credit ✓
▼			
▼			
▼			

Picklist:

BGH Ltd
Knowle plc
Purchases
Purchases ledger control
Purchases returns
RL Turner
Sales
Sales ledger control
Sales returns
Stockley & Co
VAT

Task 1.2

The following credit transactions all took place on 30 June and have been entered into the purchases returns day book as shown below. No entries have yet been made into the ledgers.

Purchases returns day book

Date 20XX	Details	Credit note number	Total £	VAT £	Net £
30 Jun	Edwards plc	C176	1,920	320	1,600
30 Jun	HJ Williams	126	1,152	192	960
	Totals		3,072	512	2,560

(a) **What will be the entries in the purchases ledger?**

Purchases Ledger

Account name	Amount £	Debit ✓	Credit ✓
▼			
▼			

(b) **What will be the entries in the general ledger?**

General ledger

Account name	Amount £	Debit ✓	Credit ✓
▼			
▼			
▼			

Picklist:

Edwards plc
HJ Williams
Purchases
Purchases ledger control
Purchases returns
Sales
Sales ledger control
Sales returns
VAT

Task 1.3

The following transactions all took place on 30 June and have been entered into the cash book as shown below. No entries have yet been made into the ledgers.

Cash book

Date 20XX	Details	Discounts £	Bank £	Date 20XX	Details	Bank £
30 Jun	JL King (credit customer)	60	2,290	30 Jun	Balance b/d	280
30 Jun	Balance c/d		30	30 Jun	Drawings by owner	1,600
				30 Jun	Motor repairs (Ignore VAT)	440
		60	2,320			2,320
				1 Jul	Balance b/d	30

(a) **What will be the TWO entries in the sales ledger?**

Sales ledger

Account name	Amount £	Debit ✓	Credit ✓
▼			
▼			

(b) **What will be the FIVE entries in the general ledger?**

General ledger

Account name	Amount £	Debit ✓	Credit ✓
▼			
▼			
▼			
▼			
▼			

Picklist:

Capital
Discounts allowed
Discounts received
Drawings
JL King
Motor vehicle expenses
Motor vehicles
Purchases ledger control
Sales ledger control

Task 1.4

Gold Ltd maintains a petty cash book as a book of prime entry; it is not part of the double entry accounting system. The following transactions all took place on 30 June and have been entered into the petty cash book as shown below. No entries have yet been made into the general ledger.

Petty cash book

Date 20XX	Details	Amount £	Date 20XX	Details	Amount £	VAT £	Office expenses £	Travel expenses	Other operating costs £
30 Jun	Opening balance	80.00	30 Jun	Envelopes	19.68	3.28	16.40		
			30 Jun	Taxi	14.00			14.00	
			30 Jun	Pens/pencils	8.16	1.36	6.80		
			30 Jun	Tea/coffee	10.80				10.80
			30 Jun	Closing balance	27.36				
		80.00			80.00	4.64	23.20	14.00	10.80

What will be the FIVE entries in the general ledger?

General ledger

Account name	Amount £	Debit ✓	Credit ✓
▼			
▼			
▼			
▼			
▼			

Picklist:

Bank
Closing balance
Envelopes
Office expenses
Opening balance
Other operating costs
Pens/pencils
Petty cash control
Taxi
Tea/coffee
Travel expenses
VAT

Task 1.5

The following two accounts are in the general ledger at the close of day on 30 June.

(a) **Insert the balance carried down together with date and details.**

(b) **Insert the totals.**

(c) **Insert the balance brought down together with date and details.**

Rent and rates

Date 20XX	Details	Amount £	Date 20XX	Details	Amount £
2 Jun	Bank	470	26 Jun	Bank	46
18 Jun	Bank	1,215		▼	
	Total			Total	
		▼			▼

Picklist:

Balance b/d
Balance c/d
Bank
Rent and rates

Wages

Date 20XX	Details	Amount £	Date 20XX	Details	Amount £
8 Jun	Bank	636		▼	
16 Jun	Bank	747		▼	
24 Jun	Bank	691		▼	
	Total			Total	
		▼			▼

Picklist:

Balance b/d
Balance c/d
Bank
Wages

Task 1.6

Below is a list of balances to be transferred to the trial balance on 30 June.

Place the figures in the debit or credit column, as appropriate, and total each column. Do not enter figures with decimal places in this task.

Account name	Amount £	Debit £	Credit £
Administration expenses	2,340		
Bank charges	136		
Bank overdraft	1,986		
Capital	37,000		
Cash in hand	454		
Commission received	200		
Discounts allowed	984		
Discounts received	1,196		
Electricity	1,640		
General expenses	2,890		
Insurance	762		
Journals and trade magazines	270		
Machinery	12,650		
Motor vehicles	18,900		
Motor vehicle expenses	530		
Purchases	27,689		
Purchases ledger control	13,965		
Purchases returns	1,540		
Rent and rates	2,519		
Sales	45,760		
Sales ledger control	19,650		
Sales returns	1,490		
VAT owing from HM Revenue & Customs	1,870		
Wages	6,873		
Totals			

Section 2

Task 2.1

Three purchases invoice have been received and partially entered in the purchases day book, as shown below.

(a) **Complete the first two entries in the purchases day book by inserting the missing figures.**

(b) **Complete the final entry in the purchases day book by inserting the appropriate figures from the following invoice.**

JJ Traders
5 Vincent Road, Darton, DF6 9HY
VAT Registration No. 217 8421 00

Invoice No. 239

To: Gold Ltd
     14 High Street
     Darton DF11 4GX

30 June 20XX

	£
400 items of product AB @ £0.75 each	300.00
400 items of product JK @ £1.10 each	220.00
	520.00
VAT @ 20%	104.00
Total	624.00

Terms: 30 days net

Purchases day book

Date 20XX	Details	Invoice number	Total £	VAT £	Net £	Product AB £	Product JK £
30 Jun	T Moxon	1032		720		3,600	
30 Jun	Lyle plc	X211			1,200		450
30 Jun	JJ Traders	239					

Task 2.2

On 10 July Gold Ltd received goods from a supplier, Perry Ltd, and an invoice for the full order. As the delivery was incomplete, Perry Ltd subsequently issued a credit note to correct the invoice.

The purchase order, goods received note and the credit note from Perry Ltd are shown below.

Gold Ltd 14 High Street Darton, DF11 4GX **Purchase Order No. 217JL**
To: Perry Ltd   Date: 6 July 20XX
Please supply: ...
600 items of product B47 @ £0.55 each
250 items of product N74 @ £1.20 each
Less 4% trade discount, as agreed.

Goods Received Note Date: 10 July 20XX GRN number: 1156
Supplier: Perry Ltd   Order number: 217JL
Goods received: 500 items of product B47   250 items of product N74
Received by: R. Winston Checked by: J. Kelvin
Comments: Incomplete order delivered.

Perry Ltd 78 Foster Street, Darton, DF3 8JU VAT Registration No. 126 3541 00 Credit Note number 129	

To: Gold Ltd
         14 High Street
         Darton DF11 4GX
	19 July 20XX

	£...
100 items of product code B47 @ £1.20 each	120.00
Less 4% trade discount	4.80
	115.20
VAT @ 20%	23.04
Total	138.24
Reason for refund: Incomplete order delivered	

(a) **Check the credit note against both the purchase order and the goods received note and complete the following sentences.**

The product code is [_____ ▼] shown on the credit note as B47.

The item price is [_____ ▼] shown on the credit note as £1.20.

The rate of trade discount is [_____ ▼] shown on the credit note as 4%.

Picklist:

correctly
incorrectly

(b) **What should have been the total amount of the credit note including VAT?**

£ [_____]

Task 2.3

Gold Ltd codes all purchases invoice with a general ledger code, a supplier account code and a product code.

Draw a line from each code below to its description.

Codes	Description
General ledger code	A code used to identify the organisation from which the goods were purchased
Supplier account code	A code used to identify the type of goods purchased
Product code	A code used to identify the account in which the purchase of the goods will be recorded

Task 2.4

Shown below is a statement of account received from a credit supplier, and the supplier's account as shown in Gold Ltd's purchases ledger.

KL Johnson Ltd						
27 Lime Grove, Darton, DF23 9LH						
To: Gold Ltd 14 High Street Darton DF11 4GX						
STATEMENT OF ACCOUNT						
Date 20XX	Invoice or credit note number	Details	Invoice amount £	Credit note amount £	Cheque amount £	Balance £
01 June		Opening balance				840
02 June		Cheque			600	240
09 June	Inv – 760	Goods	1,245			1,485
16 June	CN – 121	Goods returned		240		1,245
21 June	Inv – 801	Goods	630			1,875
28 June	Inv – 852	Goods	926			2,801

KL Johnson Ltd

Date 20XX	Details	Amount £	Date 20XX	Details	Amount £
16 Jun	Purchases returns – credit note 121	240	01 Jun	Balance b/d	240
			09 Jun	Purchases – invoice 760	1,245
			21 Jun	Purchases – invoice 801	630

(a) **Calculate the balance on the supplier's account in Gold Ltd's purchases ledger and reconcile this with the balance showing on the supplier's statement of account.**

	£
Balance on supplier's statement of account	2,801
Balance on supplier's account in purchases ledger	
Difference	

(b) **Which item on the supplier's statement of account has not yet been entered in the supplier's account in Gold Ltd's purchases ledger?**

Items	✓
Cheque for £600	
Invoice number 760	
Credit note number 121	
Invoice number 801	
Invoice number 852	

Task 2.5

Gold Ltd makes payments to suppliers by BACS on the 24th of every month and includes all items outstanding for more that 10 days.

Below is a pre-printed remittance advice slip taken from a statement of account received from a supplier, Freeman plc, showing all items outstanding.

Complete the remittance advice ready for the next payment to Freeman plc.

Remittance advice			
To: Freeman Ltd			
From: Gold Ltd			
Payment method: [▼]		Date of payment: [▼]	
The following payment will reach your bank account within three working days.			

Items outstanding			Tick if included in payment ✓
Date 20XX	Details	Amount £	
22 June	Invoice 376	650	
05 July	Credit note 28	119	
12 July	Invoice 421	544	
18 July	Invoice 488	936	
		Total amount paid £	

Picklist for payment method:

BACS
Cash
Cheque

Picklist for date of payment:

24 June 20XX
24 July 20XX
24 August 20XX

Task 2.6

On 15 July Gold Ltd delivered the goods below to a credit customer, Jack Martin, and invoice number 876 was issued the same day.

Gold Ltd
14 High Street, Darton, DF11 4GX

Delivery note No. 2176   8 July 20XX

Jack Martin   Customer account code: MAR22
20 The Hill, Highford
Warwickshire, WK7 5BS

200 units of product code B867
300 units of product code B868

On 22 July the customer returned 40 units of product code B867 as faulty. The list price of the goods was £2.60 per unit plus VAT and the customer had been given a 5% trade discount.

(a) **Complete the credit note below to two decimal places.**

CREDIT NOTE

Gold Ltd
14 High Street, Darton, DF11 4GX
VAT Registration No. 298 3827 04

To: Jack Martin   Credit note number: 267
        20 The Hill   Date: 22 July 20XX
        Highford
        Warwickshire   Customer account code: MAR22
        WK7 5BS

                                                                                        £

☐ units of product code [   ] × £ [   ] each   [   ]

                                                 Trade discount   [   ]

                                                 Net   [   ]

                                                 VAT @ 20%   [   ]

                                                 Total   [   ]

Reason for return: Faulty goods supplied on invoice number 876

Below is a selection of the general ledger account codes used by Gold Ltd.

General ledger account	Code
Sales product code B866	GL26
Sales product code B867	GL28
Sales product code B868	GL30
Sales returns product code B866	GL27
Sales returns product code B867	GL29
Sales returns product code B868	GL31

(b) **Which general ledger account code would be used to code the credit note sent to Jack Martin?**

Code	✓
GL26	
GL27	
GL28	
GL29	
GL30	
GL31	

Task 2.7

Gold Ltd sends statements of account to credit customers at the end of the month.

On 1 July, Katy Clark, a credit customer, owed Gold Ltd £865.

On 23 July, Katy Clark sent a cheque for £500 to Gold Ltd.

During July, Gold Ltd sent Katy Clark a sales invoice and a sales credit note as shown below.

Invoices issued				Credit note issued		
Date	Invoice number	Amount £		Date	Credit note number	Amount £
08 July	1574	790		17 July	387	440
28 July	1685	1,198				

(a) **Use the drag items below to enter the details and transaction amounts in the statement of account.**

(b) **Complete the final column of the statement of account.**

STATEMENT OF ACCOUNT

Gold Ltd
14 High Street, Darton, DF11 4GX.

To: Katy Clark   Date: 31 July 20XX

Date 20XX	Details and transaction amount	Outstanding amount £
01 July		
08 July		
17 July		
23 July		
28 July		

The drag and drop choices are:

Cheque	– £500
Credit note 387	– £440
Invoice 1574	– £790
Invoice 1685	– £1,198
Opening balance	

• •

Task 2.8

Below are:

• Details of invoices sent to credit customers during July, and
• Details of the payments received from each customer.

Invoice details			
Customer	Invoice date 20XX	Invoice amount	Settlement discount offered
Briggs plc	10 July	£460.00 plus VAT of £90.16	2% for payment within 14 days
Carroll Ltd	17 July	£1,360.00 plus VAT of £258.40	5% for payment within 10 days
HJ Wilks	22 July	£870.00 plus VAT of £160.08	8% for payment within 7 days

Payment details		
Customer	Date payment received 20XX	Payment amount £
Briggs plc	23 July	527.16
Carroll Ltd	31 July	1,618.40
HJ Wilks	28 July	960.48

Drag the items below to place the customer's name against the action taken by that customer.

You will not need to use all the actions.

Action taken	Customer
Customer did not pay within the specified time but still took the discount.	
Customer did not pay within the specified time and did not take the discount.	
Customer paid within the specified time and calculated the discount correctly.	
Customer paid within the specified time but calculated the discount incorrectly.	

The drag and drop choices are:
Briggs plc
Carroll Ltd
HJ Wilks

....

Task 2.9

Expenditure can be classified as capital expenditure or revenue expenditure.

(a) **Draw a line from each payment below to the appropriate form of expenditure.**

Payments	Expenditure

A payment of £1,200 to redecorate the offices	
	Capital expenditure
A payment of £20 for a new door lock	
A payment of £6,500 for new office furniture	
	Revenue expenditure
A regular payment of £2,800 for wages	

Income received can be classified as revenue income or capital income.

(b) **Complete the following sentences.**

A refund of rates paid is classified as [▼] income.

Income from the sale of old office furniture is classified as [▼] income.

Picklist:

capital
revenue

Task 2.10

Gold Ltd has general ledger accounts which can be classified as assets or liabilities.

(a) **Draw a line from each of the accounts below to the appropriate right hand box.**

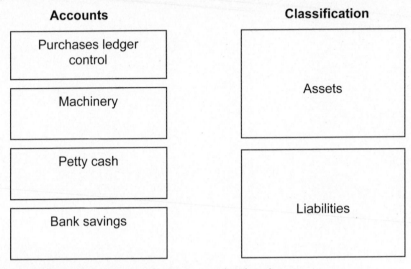

Accounts	Classification
Purchases ledger control	
Machinery	Assets
Petty cash	
Bank savings	Liabilities

Gold Ltd has bought a motor vehicle, paying by cheque.

(b) **Complete the sentence below to show how this transaction will affect the assets of Gold Ltd.**

The asset of motor vehicle will [▼] and the asset of bank will [▼]

Picklist:

increase
decrease

AAT PRACTICE ASSESSMENT 3
BASIC ACCOUNTING I

ANSWERS

Basic Accounting I AAT practice assessment 3 answers

Section 1

Task 1.1

(a)

Sales ledger

Account name	Amount £	Debit ✓	Credit ✓
BGH Ltd	4,320	✓	
Stockley & Co	1,296	✓	
RL Turner	2,544	✓	
Knowle plc	1,008	✓	

(b)

General ledger

Account name	Amount £	Debit ✓	Credit ✓
Sales ledger control	9,168	✓	
Sales	7,640		✓
VAT	1,528		✓

Task 1.2

(a)

Account name	Amount £	Debit ✓	Credit ✓
Edwards plc	1,920	✓	
HJ Williams	1,152	✓	

(b)

General ledger

Account name	Amount £	Debit ✓	Credit ✓
Purchases ledger control	3,072	✓	
Purchases returns	2,560		✓
VAT	512		✓

Task 1.3

(a)

Sales ledger

Account name	Amount £	Debit ✓	Credit ✓
JL King	2,290		✓
JL King	60		✓

(b)

General ledger

Account name	Amount £	Debit ✓	Credit ✓
Discounts allowed	60	✓	
Drawings	1,600	✓	
Motor vehicle expenses	440	✓	
Sales ledger control	2,290		✓
Sales ledger control	60		✓

Task 1.4

General ledger

Account name	Amount £	Debit ✓	Credit ✓
VAT	4.64	✓	
Office expenses	23.20	✓	
Travel expenses	14.00	✓	
Other operating costs	10.80	✓	
Petty cash control	52.64		✓

Task 1.5

Rent and rates

Date 20XX	Details	Amount £	Date 20XX	Details	Amount £
2 Jun	Bank	470	26 Jun	Bank	46
18 Jun	Bank	1,215	30 Jun	Balance c/d	1,639
	Total	1,685		Total	1,685
1 Jul	Balance b/d	1,639			

Wages

Date 20XX	Details	Amount £	Date 20XX	Details	Amount £
8 Jun	Bank	636	30 Jun	Balance c/d	2,074
16 Jun	Bank	747			
24 Jun	Bank	691			
	Total	2,074		Total	2,074
1 Jul	Balance b/d	2,074			

Task 1.6

Account name	Amount £	Debit	Credit
Administration expenses	2,340	2,340	
Bank charges	136	136	
Bank overdraft	1,986		1,986
Capital	37,000		37,000
Cash in hand	454	454	
Commission received	200		200
Discounts allowed	984	984	
Discounts received	1,196		1,196
Electricity	1,640	1,640	
General expenses	2,890	2,890	
Insurance	762	762	
Journals and trade magazines	270	270	
Machinery	12,650	12,650	
Motor vehicles	18,900	18,900	
Motor vehicle expenses	530	530	
Purchases	27,689	27,689	
Purchases ledger control	13,965		13,965
Purchases returns	1,540		1,540
Rents and rates	2,519	2,519	
Sales	45,760		45,760
Sales ledger control	19,650	19,650	
Sales returns	1,490	1,490	
VAT owing from HM Revenue & Customs	1,870	1,870	
Wages	6,873	6,873	
Totals		101,647	101,647

Section 2

Task 2.1

Purchases day book

Date 20XX	Details	Invoice Number	Total £	VAT £	Net £	Product AB £	Product JK £
30 Jun	T Moxon	1032	4,320	720	3,600	3,600	
30 Jun	Lyle plc	X211	1,440	240	1,200	750	450
30 Jun	JJ Traders	239	624	104	520	300	220

Task 2.2

(a)

The product code is [correctly] shown on the credit note as B47.

The item price is [incorrectly] shown on the credit note as £1.20.

The rate of trade discount is [correctly] shown on the credit note as 4%.

(b) The correct answer is: £63.36

Working	£
100 items of product code B47 @ £0.55 each	55.00
Less 4% trade discount (55 × 4/100)	2.20
	52.80
VAT @ 20% (52.80 × 20/100)	10.56
Total	63.36

Task 2.3

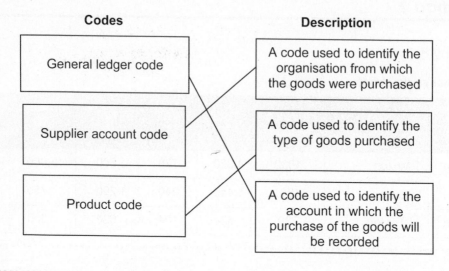

Codes	Description
General ledger code	A code used to identify the organisation from which the goods were purchased
Supplier account code	A code used to identify the type of goods purchased
Product code	A code used to identify the account in which the purchase of the goods will be recorded

Task 2.4

(a)

	£
Balance on supplier's statement of account	2,801
Balance on supplier's account in purchases ledger	1,875
Difference	926

(b)   The correct answer is: invoice number 852

Task 2.5

Remittance advice			

To: Freeman Ltd

From: Gold Ltd

Payment method: BACS   Date of payment: 24 July 20XX

The following payment will reach your bank account within three working days.

Items outstanding			Tick if included in payment ✓
Date 20XX	Details	Amount £	
22 June	Invoice 376	650	✓
05 July	Credit note 28	119	✓
12 July	Invoice 421	544	✓
18 July	Invoice 488	936	
		Total amount paid £	1,075

Task 2.6

(a)

CREDIT NOTE

Gold Ltd
14 High Street, Darton, DF11 4GX
VAT Registration No. 298 3827 04

To: Jack Martin
      20 The Hill
      Highford
      Warwickshire
      WK7 5BS

Credit note number: 267
Date: 22 July 20XX

Customer account code: MAR22

£

40 units of product code B867	× £ 2.60 each		104.00
	Trade discount		5.20
	Net		98.80
	VAT @ 20%		19.76
	Total		118.56

Reason for return: Faulty goods supplied on invoice number 876

(b)   The correct answer is: GL29

Task 2.7

<table>
<tr><td colspan="3" align="center">**STATEMENT OF ACCOUNT**</td></tr>
<tr><td colspan="3" align="center">Gold Ltd
14 High Street, Darton, DF11 4GX.</td></tr>
<tr><td colspan="2">To: Katy Clark</td><td>Date: 31 July 20XX</td></tr>
</table>

Date 20XX	Details and transaction amount	Outstanding amount £
01 July	Opening balance	865
08 July	Invoice 1,574 – £790	1,655
17 July	Credit note 387 – £440	1,215
23 July	Cheque – £500	715
28 July	Invoice 1,685 – £1,198	1,913

Task 2.8

Action taken	Customer
Customer did not pay within the specified time but still took the discount.	
Customer did not pay within the specified time and did not take the discount.	Carroll Ltd
Customer paid within the specified time and calculated the discount correctly.	HJ Wilks
Customer paid within the specified time but calculated the discount incorrectly.	Briggs plc

Task 2.9

(a)

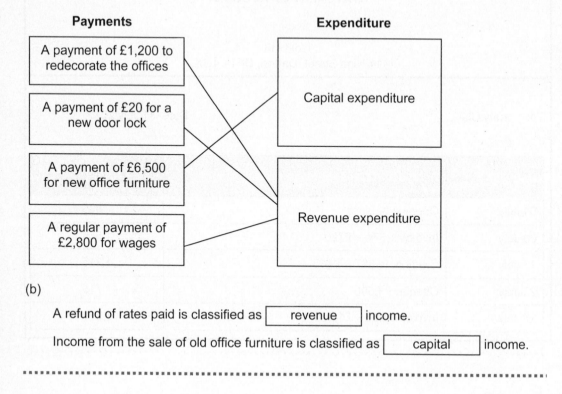

Payments	Expenditure
A payment of £1,200 to redecorate the offices	Capital expenditure
A payment of £20 for a new door lock	
A payment of £6,500 for new office furniture	Revenue expenditure
A regular payment of £2,800 for wages	

(b)

A refund of rates paid is classified as [revenue] income.

Income from the sale of old office furniture is classified as [capital] income.

Task 2.10

(a)

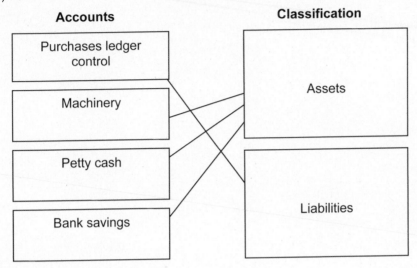

Accounts	Classification
Purchases ledger control	Assets
Machinery	
Petty cash	Liabilities
Bank savings	

(b)

The asset of motor vehicle will [increase] and the asset of bank will [decrease].

BPP PRACTICE ASSESSMENT 1
BASIC ACCOUNTING I

Time allowed: 2 hours

Basic Accounting I BPP practice assessment 1: Trappic Ltd

Trappic Ltd sells cleaning materials and equipment.

All answers should be rounded to the nearest penny unless otherwise instructed.

Section 1

Task 1.1

The following transactions all took place on 30 June and have been entered into the sales day book as shown below. No entries have yet been made into the ledger system.

Sales day book

Date 20XX	Details	Invoice number	Total £	VAT @ 20% £	Net £
30 Jun	Trilby & Co	5264	3,936	656	3,280
30 Jun	R Strang Ltd	5265	1,776	296	1,480
30 Jun	Edwards plc	5266	12,528	2,088	10,440
30 Jun	Middleton Sumner Ltd	5267	7,152	1,192	5,960
	Totals		25,392	4,232	21,160

(a) **What will be the entries in the sales ledger?**

Sales ledger

Account name	Amount £	Debit ✓	Credit ✓
▼			
▼			
▼			
▼			

Picklist:

Edwards plc
Middleton Sumner Ltd
Purchases
Purchases ledger control
Purchases returns
R Strang Ltd
Sales
Sales ledger control
Sales returns
Trilby & Co
VAT

(b) **What will be the entries in the general ledger?**

General ledger

Account name	Amount £	Debit ✓	Credit ✓
▼			
▼			
▼			

Picklist:

Edwards plc
Middleton Sumner Ltd
Purchases
Purchases ledger control
Purchases returns
R Strang Ltd
Sales
Sales ledger control
Sales returns
Trilby & Co
VAT

Task 1.2

The following credit transactions all took place on 30 June and have been entered into the purchases returns day book as shown below. No entries have yet been made in the ledgers.

Purchases returns day book

Date 20XX	Details	Credit note number	Total £	VAT @ 20% £	Net £
30 June	Bingley & Co	09374	672	112	560
30 June	Arkwright Ltd	CN5426	2,208	368	1,840
	Totals		2,880	480	2,400

(a) **What will be the entries in the purchases ledger?**

Purchases ledger

Account name	Amount £	Debit ✓	Credit ✓
▼			
▼			

Picklist:

Arkwright Ltd
Bingley & Co
Purchases
Purchases ledger control
Purchases returns
Sales
Sales ledger control
Sales returns
VAT

(b) **What will be the entries in the general ledger?**

General ledger

Account name	Amount £	Debit ✓	Credit ✓
▼			
▼			
▼			

Picklist:

Arkwright Ltd
Bingley & Co
Purchases
Purchases ledger control
Purchases returns
Sales
Sales ledger control
Sales returns
VAT

Task 1.3

The following transactions all took place on 30 June and have been entered in the debit side of the cash book as shown below. No entries have yet been made in the ledgers.

Cash book – Debit side

Date 20XX	Details	VAT @ 20% £	Bank £
30 Jun 30 Jun	Henderson & Co Cash sale	 71	7,349 426

(a) **What will be the entry in the sales ledger?**

Sales ledger

Account name	Amount £	Debit ✓	Credit ✓
▼			

Picklist:

Bank
Henderson & Co
Purchases ledger control
Sales
Sales ledger control
VAT

(b) **What will be the THREE entries in the general ledger?**

General ledger

Account name	Amount £	Debit ✓	Credit ✓
▼			
▼			
▼			

Picklist:

Bank
Henderson & Co
Purchases ledger control
Sales
Sales ledger control
VAT

The following transactions all took place on 30 June and have been entered in the credit side of the cash book as shown below. No entries have yet been made in the ledgers.

Cash book – Credit side

Date 20XX	Details	Discounts £	Bank £
30 Jun 30 Jun	Balance b/d Resto plc	 10	575 282

(c) **What will be the THREE entries in the general ledger?**

General ledger

Account name	Amount £	Debit ✓	Credit ✓
▼			
▼			
▼			

Picklist:

Balance b/d
Balance c/d
Bank
Discounts allowed
Discounts received
Purchases ledger control
Resto plc
Sales ledger control
VAT

Task 1.4

Trappic Ltd maintains a petty cash book as both a book of prime entry and part of the double entry accounting system. The following transactions all took place on 30 June and have been entered in the petty cash book as shown below. No entries have yet been made in the general ledger.

Petty cash book

Date 20XX	Details	Amount £	Date 20XX	Details	Amount £	VAT @ 20% £	Motor expenses £	Travel £	Office expenses £
30 Jun	Balance b/d	75.00	30 Jun 30 Jun 30 Jun 30 Jun 30 Jun	Tea/biscuits Train fare Paper Oil for car Balance c/d	7.89 23.40 48.00 21.60 199.11	 8.00 3.60	 18.00	 23.40	7.89 40.00
30 Jun	Bank	225.00							
		300.00			300.00	11.60	18.00	23.40	47.89

What will be the FIVE entries in the general ledger?

General ledger

Account name	Amount £	Debit ✓	Credit ✓
▼			
▼			
▼			
▼			
▼			

Picklist:

Balance b/d
Balance c/d
Bank
Motor expenses
Office expenses
Oil for car
Paper
Tea/biscuits
Train fare
Travel
Petty cash book
VAT

....

Task 1.5

The following two accounts are in the general ledger at the close of day on 30 June.

(a) **Insert the balance carried down together with date and details.**
(b) **Insert the totals.**
(c) **Insert the balance brought down together with date and details.**

Heat and light

Date 20XX	Details	Amount £	Date 20XX	Details	Amount £
01 Jun	Balance b/d	2,039		▾	
26 Jun	Purchases ledger control	348		▾	
	▾			▾	
	Total			Total	
	▾			▾	

Picklist:

Balance b/d
Balance c/d
Bank
Purchases ledger control

Sales

Date 20XX	Details	Amount £	Date 20XX	Details	Amount £
	▾		01 Jun	Balance b/d	32,986
	▾		22 Jun	Bank	750
	▾			▾	
	Total			Total	
	▾			▾	

Picklist:

Balance b/d
Balance c/d
Bank
Sales ledger control

....

Task 1.6

Below is a list of balances to be transferred to the trial balance as at 30 June.

Place the figures in the debit or credit column, as appropriate, and total each column.

Account name	Amount £	Debit £	Credit £
Machinery	15,000		
Inventory	3,907		
Cash at bank	1,342		
Petty cash	150		
Sales ledger control	9,486		
Purchases ledger control	4,003		
VAT owing to HM Revenue & Customs	1,880		
Capital	10,000		
Loan from bank	2,500		
Sales	86,262		
Sales returns	1,256		
Purchases	43,278		
Purchases returns	295		
Discounts received	987		
Discounts allowed	628		
Salaries	21,965		
Motor expenses	1,025		
Office expenses	1,234		
Premises costs	2,833		
Marketing expenses	765		
Travel	911		
Telephone	1,260		
Heat and light	1,387		
Rental income	500		
Totals			

Section 2

Task 2.1

Purchases invoices have been checked and partially entered in the purchases day book, as shown below.

(a) **Complete the entries in the purchases day book by inserting the appropriate figures for each invoice.**

(b) **Total the last five columns of the purchases day book.**

Purchases day book

Date 20XX	Details	Invoice number	Total £	VAT @ 20% £	Net £	Purchases £	Expenses £
30 Jun	Webble Ltd	76238		600		3,000	
30 Jun	Griddo plc	12522	288				240
30 Jun	Antic & Co	0938	816		680	680	
	Totals						

Task 2.2

A supply of cleaning fluid has been delivered to Trappic Ltd by OMKG Chemicals. The purchase order sent from Trappic Ltd, and the invoice from OMKG Chemicals, are shown below.

Trappic Ltd
8 Highview Road
Arbuckle
AR7 4LX

Purchase Order No. 637821

To: OMKG Chemicals

Date: 15 July 20XX

Please supply 1000 litres cleaning fluid product code 7638XX
Purchase price: £8.00 per 10 litres, plus VAT
Discount: less 15% trade discount, as agreed.

OMKG Chemicals
76 Grange Road, Arbuckle AR1 0HJ
VAT Registration No. 653 9922 33

Invoice No. 76383

Trappic Ltd
8 Highview Road
Arbuckle
AR7 4LX

22 July 20XX

1000 litres cleaning fluid product code 7638XX @ £0.80 per litre	£800.00
Less: trade discount at 12.5%	£100.00
	£700.00
VAT @ 20%	£140.00
Total	£840.00

Terms: 30 days net

Check the invoice against the purchase order and answer the following questions.

	Yes ✓	No ✓
Has the correct purchase price of the cleaning fluid been charged?		
Has the correct discount been applied?		
What would be the VAT amount charged if the invoice was correct?	£	
What would be the total amount charged if the invoice was correct?	£	

Task 2.3

Trappic Ltd codes all purchase invoices with a supplier code AND a general ledger code. A selection of the codes used is given below.

Supplier	Supplier Code
Bridgend plc	BRI12
Distinct Ltd	DIS53
Finish Clear & Co	FIN09
Hepplewhite Clean Ltd	HEP76
Mirrors and Glass Ltd	MIR22

Item	General Ledger Code
Cleaning fluids	GL234
Mops and buckets	GL237
Brushes	GL240
Cloths	GL244
Protective clothing	GL248

This is an invoice received from a supplier.

Distinct Ltd **89 Northcourt Road, Arbuckle AR5 3VB** **VAT Registration No. 837 4777 33**
Trappic Ltd 8 Highview Road Arbuckle AR7 4LX 22 July 20XX

10 .... Mops with buckets @ £12.60 each	£126.00
VAT @ 20%	£ 25.20
Total	£151.20

(a) **Select which codes would be used to code this invoice.**

Supplier code	▼
General ledger code	▼

Picklist:

BRI12
DIS53
FIN09
HEP76
MIR22
GL234
GL237
GL240
GL244
GL248

(b) **Why is it necessary to use a supplier code?**

Picklist:

To help trace relevant information quickly and easily
To help when ordering an item
To help find the total amount of purchases
To help when storing an item of inventory

Task 2.4

Shown below is a statement of account received from a credit supplier, and the supplier's account as shown in the purchases ledger of Trappic Ltd.

Lemonfresh Ltd
90 West Street
Arbuckle
AR4 8AM

To: Trappic Ltd
8 Highview Road
Arbuckle
AR7 4LX

STATEMENT OF ACCOUNT

Date 20XX	Invoice Number	Details	Invoice amount £	Cheque amount £	Balance £
1 May	1267	Goods	180		180
3 June	1387	Goods	230		410
7 June	1422	Goods	290		700
10 June	1498	Goods	800		1,500
16 June		Cheque		510	990

Lemonfresh Ltd

Date 20XX	Details	Amount £	Date 20XX	Details	Amount £
16 June	Bank	510	1 May	Purchases	180
16 June	Discount	10	3 June	Purchases	230
			7 June	Purchases	290

(a) **Which item is missing from the statement of account from Lemonfresh Ltd?**

Picklist:

Invoice 1267
Invoice 1387
Invoice 1422
Invoice 1498
Cheque for £510
Discount for £10

(b) **Which item is missing from the supplier account in Trappic Ltd's purchases ledger?**

▼

Picklist:

Invoice 1267
Invoice 1387
Invoice 1422
Invoice 1498
Cheque for £510
Discount for £10

(c) **Assuming any differences between the statement of account from Lemonfresh Ltd and the supplier account in Trappic Ltd's purchases ledger are simply due to omission errors, what is the amount owing to Lemonfresh Ltd?**

£	

Task 2.5

Trappic Ltd sends out cheques to suppliers on the last day of the month following the month of invoice. Below is an extract from the purchases ledger of Trappic Ltd.

Inkaway Ltd

Date 20XX	Details	Amount £	Date 20XX	Details	Amount £
21 May	Purchases returns (credit note 542)	199	7 May	Purchases invoice 6735	3,289
14 June	Purchases returns (credit note 599)	158	2 June	Purchases Invoice 6890	4,700
30 June	Bank	3,090	13 July	Purchases Invoice 6913	3,690

(a) **Complete the remittance advice note for Trappic Ltd's payment to the supplier on 31 July 20XX.**

Trappic Ltd
8 Highview Road
Arbuckle
AR7 4LX

REMITTANCE ADVICE

To: Inkaway Ltd   Date: 31 July 20XX

Please find attached our cheque in payment of the following amounts.

Invoice number	Credit note number	Amount £
	Total amount paid	

(b) **Which of the following statements is true?**

	✓
The remittance advice note will be sent to the customer to advise them of the amount being paid	
The remittance advice note will be sent to the supplier's bank to advise them of the amount being paid	
The remittance advice note will be sent to the supplier to advise them of the amount being paid	
The remittance advice note will be sent to the accounts department at Inkaway Ltd to request that a cheque is raised	

Task 2.6

On 5 July Trappic Ltd delivered the following goods to a credit customer, Nemesis Ltd.

Trappic Ltd

8 Highview Road
Arbuckle
AR7 4LX

Delivery note No. 8793
05 July 20XX

Nemesis Ltd   Customer account code: NEM893
36 Ventnor Road
Arbuckle
AR7 9LC

200 polishing cloths, product code C420.

The list price of the goods was £0.50 per cloth plus VAT. Nemesis Ltd is to be given a 10% trade discount and a 4% early settlement discount.

(a) **Complete the invoice below.**

Trappic Ltd
8 Highview Road
Arbuckle
AR7 4LX

VAT Registration No. 782 8723 23

Nemesis Ltd   Customer account code: NEM893

36 Ventnor Road
Arbuckle
AR7 9LC
Date: 6 July 20XX

Invoice No: 67282
Delivery note number: 8793

Quantity of goods	Product code	Total list price £	Net amount after trade discount £	VAT £	Gross £

Trappic Ltd offers each customer a discount of 5% if any order amounts to £1,000 or over.

(b) **What is the name of this type of discount?**

[▼]

Picklist:

Bulk discount
Settlement discount
Trade discount

Task 2.7

The following is a summary of transactions with Quemix Ltd, a new credit customer.

£1,020 re invoice 67300 of 11 July
£987 re invoice 67400 of 19 July
£48 re credit note 5640 of 24 July
£2,967 re invoice 67500 of 28 July
Cheque for £1,020 received 31 July

Complete the statement of account below.

Trappic Ltd
8 Highview Road
Arbuckle
AR7 4LX

To: Quemix Ltd   Date: 31 July 20XX

Date 20XX	Details	Transaction amount £	Outstanding amount £
11 July	Invoice 67300		
19 July	Invoice 67400		
24 July	Credit note 5640		
28 July	Invoice 67500		
31 July	Cheque		

Task 2.8

The account shown below is in the sales ledger of Trappic Ltd. A cheque for £2,311 has now been received from this customer.

Sibley & Co

Date 20XX	Details	Amount £	Date 20XX	Details	Amount £
1 May	Balance b/d	2,897	2 June	Sales returns credit note 5530	173
3 June	Sales invoice 66100	2,556	25 June	Bank	2,724
28 June	Sales Invoice 66800	2,453	26 June	Sales returns credit note 5570	245

(a) **Which outstanding item has not been included in the payment of £2,311?**

▼

Picklist:

Balance b/d
Sales invoice 66100
Sales invoice 66800
Bank
Sales returns credit note 5530
Sales returns credit note 5570

An invoice is being prepared to be sent to Sibley & Co for £760.00 plus VAT of £144.40. A settlement discount of 5% will be offered for payment within 10 days.

(b) **What is the amount Trappic Ltd should receive if payment is made within 10 days?**

£

(c) **What is the amount Trappic Ltd should receive if payment is NOT made within 10 days?**

£

....

Task 2.9

It is important to understand the difference between capital expenditure, revenue expenditure, capital income and revenue income.

Select one option in each instance below to show whether the item will be capital expenditure, revenue expenditure, capital income or revenue income.

Item	Capital expenditure ✓	Revenue expenditure ✓	Capital income ✓	Revenue income ✓
Purchase of mops and buckets for resale				
Receipt from sale of an item of Trappic Ltd's machinery				
Purchase of delivery vehicle				
Cash purchases				
Payments to credit suppliers				
Sale of goods for cash				

Task 2.10

Financial accounting is based upon the accounting equation.

(a) **Show whether the following statements are True or False.**

	True ✓	False ✓
Income less expenditure is equal to assets		
Capital plus liabilities are equal to assets		
Liabilities equal assets plus capital		

(b) **Classify each of the following items as an asset, a liability or capital.**

Item	Asset, liability or capital?
Money contributed by the owners	▼
Bank overdraft	▼
Petty cash	▼

Picklist:

Asset
Liability
Capital

BPP PRACTICE ASSESSMENT 1
BASIC ACCOUNTING I

ANSWERS

Basic Accounting I BPP practice assessment 1: Trappic Ltd

Section 1

Task 1.1

(a)

Sales ledger

Account name	Amount £	Debit ✓	Credit ✓
Edwards plc	12,528	✓	
Middleton Sumner Ltd	7,152	✓	
R Strang Ltd	1,776	✓	
Trilby & Co	3,936	✓	

(b)

General ledger

Account name	Amount £	Debit ✓	Credit ✓
Sales	21,160		✓
Sales ledger control	25,392	✓	
VAT	4,232		✓

Task 1.2

(a)

Purchases ledger

Account name	Amount £	Debit ✓	Credit ✓
Arkwright Ltd	2,208	✓	
Bingley & Co	672	✓	

(b)

General ledger

Account name	Amount £	Debit ✓	Credit ✓
Purchases ledger control	2,880	✓	
Purchases returns	2,400		✓
VAT	480		✓

Task 1.3

(a)

Sales ledger

Account name	Amount £	Debit ✓	Credit ✓
Henderson & Co	7,349		✓

(b)

Sales ledger

Account name	Amount £	Debit ✓	Credit ✓
Sales ledger control	7,349		✓
Sales	355		✓
VAT	71		✓

(c)

General ledger

Account name	Amount £	Debit ✓	Credit ✓
Purchases ledger control	282	✓	
Purchases ledger control	10	✓	
Discounts received	10		✓

Task 1.4

General ledger

Account name	Amount £	Debit ✓	Credit ✓
Bank	225.00		✓
Motor expenses	18.00	✓	
Office expenses	47.89	✓	
Travel	23.40	✓	
VAT	11.60	✓	

Task 1.5

(a) – (c)

Heat and light

Date 20XX	Details	Amount £	Date 20XX	Details	Amount £
01 Jun	Balance b/d	2,039			
26 Jun	Purchases ledger control	348			
			30 Jun	Balance c/d	2,387
	Total	2,387		Total	2,387
1 Jul	Balance b/d	2,387			

Sales

Date 20XX	Details	Amount £	Date 20XX	Details	Amount £
			01 Jun	Balance b/d	32,986
			22 Jun	Bank	750
30 Jun	Balance c/d	33,736			
	Total	33,736		Total	33,736
			1 Jul	Balance b/d	33,786

Task 1.6

Account name	Amount £	Debit £	Credit £
Machinery	15,000	15,000	
Inventory	3,907	3,907	
Cash at bank	1,342	1,342	
Petty cash	150	150	
Sales ledger control	9,486	9,486	
Purchases ledger control	4,003		4,003
VAT owing to HM Revenue & Customs	1,880		1,880
Capital	10,000		10,000
Loan from bank	2,500		2,500
Sales	86,262		86,262
Sales returns	1,256	1,256	
Purchases	43,278	43,278	
Purchases returns	295		295
Discounts received	987		987
Discounts allowed	628	628	
Salaries	21,965	21,965	
Motor expenses	1,025	1,025	
Office expenses	1,234	1,234	
Premises costs	2,833	2,833	
Marketing expenses	765	765	
Travel	911	911	
Telephone	1,260	1,260	
Heat and light	1,387	1,387	
Rental income	500		500
Totals		106,427	106,427

Section 2

Task 2.1

(a) and (b)

Purchases day book

Date 20XX	Details	Invoice number	Total £	VAT £	Net £	Purchases £	Expenses £
30 Jun	Webble Ltd	76238	3,600	600	3,000	3,000	
30 Jun	Griddo plc	12522	288	48	240		240
30 Jun	Antic & Co	0938	816	136	680	680	
	Totals		4,704	784	3,920	3,680	240

Task 2.2

VAT: (800 – (800 × 15/100)) × 20/100 = 136

Total: (800 – (800 × 15/100)) + 136 = 816

	Yes ✓	No ✓
Has the correct purchase price of the cleaning fluid been charged?	✓	
Has the correct discount been applied?		✓
What would be the VAT amount charged if the invoice was correct?	£	136
What would be the total amount charged if the invoice was correct?	£	816

Task 2.3

(a)

Supplier code	DIS53
General ledger code	GL237

(b)   The correct answer is: to help trace relevant information quickly and easily

Task 2.4

(a) The correct answer is: discount for £10

(b) The correct answer is: invoice 1498

(c) The correct answer is: £980

£990 – £10 = £980

Task 2.5

(a)

Trappic Ltd		
8 Highview Road		
Arbuckle		
AR7 4LX		

REMITTANCE ADVICE

To: Inkaway Ltd 20XX

Date: 31 July

Please find attached our cheque in payment of the following amounts.

Invoice number	Credit note number	Amount £
6890		4,700
	599	158
	Total amount paid	4,542

(b) The correct answer is: the remittance advice note will be sent to the supplier to advise them of the amount being paid

---

Task 2.6

(a) VAT: (90 – (90 × 4/100)) × 20/100 = £17.28

Trappic Ltd 8 Highview Road Arbuckle AR7 4LX					

VAT Registration No. 782 8723 23

Nemesis Ltd   Customer account code: NEM893
36 Ventnor Road
Arbuckle
AR7 9LC

Date: 6 July 20XX

Invoice No: 67282
Delivery note number: 8793

Quantity of goods	Product code	Total list price £	Net amount after trade discount £	VAT £	Gross £
200	C420	100.00	90.00	17.28	107.28

(b) The correct answer is: bulk discount

Task 2.7

Trappic Ltd
8 Highview Road
Arbuckle
AR7 4LX

To: Quemix Ltd   Date: 31 July 20XX

Date 20XX	Details	Transaction amount £	Outstanding amount £
11 July	Invoice 67300	1,020	1,020
19 July	Invoice 67400	987	2,007
24 July	Credit note 5640	48	1,959
28 July	Invoice 67500	2,967	4,926
31 July	Cheque	1,020	3,906

Task 2.8

(a) The correct answer is: sales invoice 66800

(b) The correct answer is: £866.40

Working

(£760.00 × 95%) + £144.40 = £866.40

(c) The correct answer is: £904.40

Working

(£760.00 + £144.40 = £904.40)

Task 2.9

Item	Capital expenditure ✓	Revenue expenditure ✓	Capital income ✓	Revenue income ✓
Purchase of mops and buckets for resale		✓		
Receipt from sale of an item of Trappic Ltd's machinery			✓	
Purchase of delivery vehicle	✓			
Cash purchases		✓		
Payments to credit suppliers		✓		
Sale of goods for cash				✓

Task 2.10

(a)

	True ✓	False ✓
Income less expenditure is equal to assets		✓
Capital plus liabilities are equal to assets	✓	
Liabilities equal assets plus capital		✓

(b)

Item	Asset, liability or capital?
Money contributed by the owners	Capital
Bank overdraft	Liability
Petty cash	Asset

BPP PRACTICE ASSESSMENT 2
BASIC ACCOUNTING I

Time allowed: 2 hours

PRACTICE ASSESSMENT 2

Basic Accounting I BPP practice assessment 2: Hazelcombe & Co

Hazelcombe & Co sells vehicle parts to garages and car manufacturers.

All answers should be rounded to the nearest penny unless otherwise instructed.

Section 1

Task 1.1

The following transactions all took place on 30 June and have been entered into the purchases day book as shown below. No entries have yet been made into the ledger system.

Purchases day book

Date 20XX	Details	Invoice number	Total £	VAT @ 20% £	Net £
30 Jun	Osman Ltd	2764	2,688	448	2,240
30 Jun	Foster Brothers	I546/20	1,536	256	1,280
30 Jun	Lindemann plc	67383	5,328	888	4,440
30 Jun	Stoke Rows Ltd	412	3,840	640	3,200
	Totals		13,392	2,232	11,160

(a) **What will be the entries in the purchases ledger?**

Purchases ledger

Account name	Amount £	Debit ✓	Credit ✓
▼			
▼			
▼			
▼			

Picklist:

Foster Brothers
Lindemann plc
Purchases
Purchases ledger control
Purchases returns

Osman Ltd
Sales
Sales ledger control
Sales returns
Stoke Rows Ltd
VAT

(b) **What will be the entries in the general ledger?**

General ledger

Account name		Amount £	Debit ✓	Credit ✓
	▼			
	▼			
	▼			

Picklist:

Foster Brothers
Lindemann plc
Purchases
Purchases ledger control
Purchases returns
Osman Ltd
Sales
Sales ledger control
Sales returns
Stoke Rows Ltd
VAT

Task 1.2

The following credit transactions all took place on 30 June and have been entered into the sales returns day book as shown below. No entries have yet been made in the ledgers.

Sales returns day book

Date 20XX	Details	Credit note number	Total £	VAT @ 20% £	Net £
30 June	Austen Knight plc	CN876	144	24	120
30 June	Tristram Steers & Co	CN877	2,832	472	2,360
	Totals		2,976	496	2,480

(a) **What will be the entries in the sales ledger?**

Sales ledger

Account name	Amount £	Debit ✓	Credit ✓
▼			
▼			

Picklist:

Austen Knight plc
Purchases
Purchases ledger control
Purchases returns
Sales
Sales ledger control
Sales returns
Tristram Steers & Co
VAT

(b) **What will be the entries in the general ledger?**

General ledger

Account name	Amount £	Debit ✓	Credit ✓
▼			
▼			
▼			

Picklist:

Austen Knight plc
Purchases
Purchases ledger control
Purchases returns
Sales
Sales ledger control
Sales returns
Tristram Steers & Co
VAT

Task 1.3

The following transactions all took place on 30 June and have been entered in the debit side of the cash book as shown below. No entries have yet been made in the ledgers.

Cash book – Debit side

Date 20XX	Details	Discounts £	Bank £
30 Jun	Gwendolin Ltd	15	643
30 Jun	Marcham & Co		2,309
		15	2,952

(a) **What will be the THREE entries in the sales ledger?**

Sales ledger

Account name	Amount £	Debit ✓	Credit ✓
▼			
▼			
▼			

Picklist:

Bank
Discounts allowed
Discounts received
Gwendolin Ltd
Marcham & Co
Purchases
Purchases ledger control
Sales
Sales ledger control
VAT

(b) **What will be the THREE entries in the general ledger?**

General ledger

Account name	Amount £	Debit ✓	Credit ✓
▼			
▼			
▼			

Picklist:

Bank
Discounts allowed
Discounts received
Gwendolin Ltd
Marcham & Co
Purchases
Purchases ledger control
Sales
Sales ledger control
VAT

The following transactions took place on 30 June and has been entered in the credit side of the cash book as shown below. No entries have yet been made in the ledgers.

Cash book – Credit side

Date 20XX	Details	VAT @ 20% £	Bank £
30 Jun	Bradfield & Co		2,385
30 Jun	Cash purchase	40	240

(c) **What will be the entry in the purchases ledger?**

Purchases ledger

Account name	Amount £	Debit ✓	Credit ✓
▼			

Picklist:

Bank
Bradfield & Co
Discounts allowed
Discounts received
Purchases
Purchases ledger control
Sales
Sales ledger control
VAT

Task 1.4

Hazelcombe & Co maintains a petty cash book as a book of prime entry only. The following transactions all took place on 30 June and have been entered in the petty cash book as shown below. No entries have yet been made in the general ledger.

Petty cash book – Credit side

Date 20XX	Details	Amount £	VAT @ 20% £	Distribution expenses £	Travel £	Office expenses £
30 Jun	Envelopes	18.24	3.04			15.20
30 Jun	Postage	13.40				13.40
30 Jun	De-icer	6.72	1.12	5.60		
30 Jun	Bus fares	17.65			17.65	
		56.01	4.16	5.60	17.65	28.60

What will be the FIVE entries in the general ledger?

General ledger

Account name	Amount £	Debit ✓	Credit ✓
▼			
▼			
▼			
▼			
▼			

Picklist:

Bank
Bus fares
De-icer
Distribution expenses
Envelopes
Office expenses
Petty cash control
Postage
Travel
VAT

Task 1.5

The following two accounts are in the general ledger at the close of day on 30 June.

(a) **Insert the balance carried down together with date and details.**
(b) **Insert the totals.**
(c) **Insert the balance brought down together with date and details.**

Office expenses

Date 20XX	Details	Amount £	Date 20XX	Details	Amount £
01 Jun	Balance b/d	12,945		▼	
30 Jun	Petty cash	42		▼	
30 Jun	Purchases ledger control	523		▼	
	▼			▼	
	Total			Total	
	▼			▼	

Picklist:
Balance b/d
Balance c/d
Bank
Petty cash
Purchases ledger control

Commission received

Date 20XX	Details	Amount £	Date 20XX	Details	Amount £
	▼		01 Jun	Balance b/d	1,276
	▼		30 Jun	Bank	18
	▼			▼	
	Total			Total	
	▼			▼	

Picklist:
Balance b/d
Balance c/d
Bank
Petty cash
Sales ledger control

Task 1.6

Below is a list of balances to be transferred to the trial balance as at 30 June.

Place the figures in the debit or credit column, as appropriate, and total each column.

Account name	Amount £	Debit £	Credit £
Advertising	789		
Bank overdraft	2,137		
Capital	5,000		
Commission income	1,356		
Discounts allowed	1,986		
Discounts received	2,543		
Distribution expenses	9,110		
Furniture and fittings	18,750		
Inventory	12,354		
Loan from bank	10,000		
Maintenance	1,035		
Office expenses	13,728		
Petty cash	250		
Purchases	66,390		
Purchases ledger control	6,297		
Purchases returns	3,287		
Rent and rates	8,265		
Sales	172,242		
Sales ledger control	24,910		
Sales returns	2,890		
Telephone and internet	2,165		
Travel	1,023		
VAT owing to HM Revenue & Customs	5,320		
Wages and salaries	44,537		
Totals			

(a) **Which item is missing from the statement of account from SpareParts plc?**

	▼

Picklist:

Credit note C043
Invoice I893
Invoice I999
Invoice I034
Cheque for £2,395
Discount for £27

(b) **Which item is missing from the supplier account in Hazelcombe & Co's purchases ledger?**

	▼

Picklist:

Credit note C043
Invoice I893
Invoice I999
Invoice I034
Cheque for £2,395
Discount for £27

(c) **Assuming any differences between the statement of account from SpareParts plc and the supplier account in Hazelcombe & Co's purchases ledger are simply due to omission errors, what is the amount owing to SpareParts plc?**

£ [   ]

....

Task 2.5

Hazelcombe & Co sends out cheques to suppliers on the last Wednesday of the month following the month of the relevant invoice or credit note. Below is an extract from the purchases ledger of Hazelcombe & Co.

Cooper Foundry Ltd

Date 20XX	Details	Amount £	Date 20XX	Details	Amount £
29 May	Purchases returns (credit note 039)	45	25 May	Purchases invoice 09364	982
6 June	Purchases returns (credit note 124)	63	1 June	Purchases invoice 09528	2,386
29 June	Bank	937	19 July	Purchases invoice 09785	1,802

(a) **Complete the remittance advice note for Hazelcombe & Co's payment to the supplier on 27 July 20XX, the last Wednesday of July.**

Hazelcombe & Co
42 Turnstile Trading Estate
Luscombe
LU9 0FG

REMITTANCE ADVICE

To: Cooper Foundry Ltd   Date: 27 July 20XX

Please find attached our cheque in payment of the following amounts.

Invoice number	Credit note number	Amount £
	Total amount paid	

(b) Invoice number 09785 will be paid by Hazelcombe & Co in

	✓
June	
July	
August	
September	

Task 2.6

On 10 July Hazelcombe & Co delivered the following goods to a credit customer, Warriner plc.

Hazelcombe & Co
42 Turnstile Trading Estate
Luscombe
LU9 0FG

Delivery note No. 90230
10 July 20XX

Warriner plc   Customer account code: W981
45 Printer Lane
Luscombe
LU3 9LA

500 fixings, product code FX827.

The list price of the goods was £20.00 per box of 10 fixings plus VAT. Warriner plc is to be given a 20% trade discount and a 2% early settlement discount.

(a) **Complete the invoice below.**

Hazelcombe & Co
42 Turnstile Trading Estate
Luscombe
LU9 0FG

VAT Registration No. 928 2781 110

Warriner plc   Customer account code: W981
45 Printer Lane
Luscombe
LU3 9LA

                                          Date: 11 July 20XX

Invoice No: 21026
Delivery note number: 90230

Quantity of goods	Product code	Total list price £	Net amount after trade discount £	VAT £	Gross £

Hazelcombe & Co offers each customer a discount of 5% if any order amounts to £2,000 or over.

(b) **What is the name of this type of discount?**

▼

Picklist:

Bulk discount
Settlement discount
Trade discount

Task 2.7

The following is a summary of transactions with Tarsus & Co, a new credit customer.

£1,430 re invoice 21104 of 13 July
£213 re credit note 920 of 17 July
£947 re invoice 21309 of 22 July
Cheque for £1,020 received 30 July
Settlement discount £15 taken 30 July

Complete the statement of account below.

Hazelcombe & Co
42 Turnstile Trading Estate
Luscombe
LU9 0FG

To: Tarsus & Co   Date: 31 July 20XX

Date 20XX	Details	Transaction amount £	Outstanding amount £
13 July	Invoice 21104		
17 July	Credit note 920		
22 July	Invoice 21309		
30 July	Cheque		
30 July	Discount taken		

Task 2.8

The account shown below is in the sales ledger of Hazelcombe & Co. A remittance advice for an automated payment of £1,534 has now been received from this customer.

Oster Ltd

Date 20XX	Details	Amount £	Date 20XX	Details	Amount £
15 May	Sales invoice 19011	1,920	28 May	Sales returns credit note 801	84
16 June	Sales invoice 20332	1,743	15 June	Bank	1,836
17 July	Sales Invoice 21276	1,633	21 June	Sales returns credit note 893	209

(a) **Which outstanding item has not been included in the payment of £1,534?**

▼

> **Picklist:**
>
> Sales invoice 19011
> Sales invoice 20332
> Sales invoice 21276
> Bank
> Sales returns credit note 801
> Sales returns credit note 893

An invoice is being prepared to be sent Oster Ltd for £1,180.00 plus VAT of £231.28. A settlement discount of 2% will be offered for payment within 10 days.

(b) **What is the amount Hazelcombe & Co should receive if payment is made within 10 days?**

£

(c) **What is the amount Hazelcombe & Co should receive if payment is NOT made within 10 days?**

£

....

Task 2.9

It is important to understand the difference between capital expenditure, revenue expenditure, capital income and revenue income.

Select one option in each instance below to show whether the item will be capital expenditure, revenue expenditure, capital income or revenue income.

Item	Capital expenditure ✓	Revenue expenditure ✓	Capital income ✓	Revenue income ✓
Cash sales				
Purchase on credit of lights for resale				
Sale of goods on credit				
Purchase of office computer				
Payments to credit suppliers				
Receipt from sale of an item of Hazelcombe & Co's furniture and fittings				

Task 2.10

(a) **Show whether the following statements are True or False.**

	True ✓	False ✓
An increase in an asset is shown as a credit entry in the general ledger		
A decrease in liabilities is shown as a credit entry in the general ledger		
An increase in capital is shown as a credit entry in the general ledger		

(b) **Identify from the picklist an example of an asset, a liability and a capital transaction.**

Item	Example from picklist	
Asset		▼
Liability		▼
Capital transaction		▼

Picklist:

Trade receivables
Bank overdraft
Drawings

BPP PRACTICE ASSESSMENT 2
BASIC ACCOUNTING I

ANSWERS

Accounting I BPP practice assessment 2: Hazelcombe & Co

Section 1

Task 1.1

(a)

Purchases ledger

Account name	Amount £	Debit ✓	Credit ✓
Lindemann plc	5,328		✓
Stoke Rows Ltd	3,840		✓
Foster Brothers	1,536		✓
Osman Ltd	2,688		✓

(b)

General ledger

Account name	Amount £	Debit ✓	Credit ✓
Purchases	11,160	✓	
Purchases ledger control	13,392		✓
VAT	2,232	✓	

Task 1.2

(a)

Sales ledger

Account name	Amount £	Debit ✓	Credit ✓
Tristram Steers & Co	2,832		✓
Austen Knight plc	144		✓

(b)

General ledger

Account name	Amount £	Debit ✓	Credit ✓
Sales ledger control	2,976		✓
Sales returns	2,480	✓	
VAT	496	✓	

Task 1.3

(a)

Sales ledger

Account name	Amount £	Debit ✓	Credit ✓
Gwendolin Ltd	643		✓
Gwendolin Ltd	15		✓
Marcham & Co	2,309		✓

(b)

General ledger

General ledger			
Account name	Amount £	Debit ✓	Credit ✓
Sales ledger control	2,952		✓
Sales ledger control	15		✓
Discounts allowed	15	✓	

(c)

Purchases ledger

Account name	Amount £	Debit ✓	Credit ✓
Bradfield & Co	2,385	✓	

Task 1.4

General ledger

Account name	Amount £	Debit ✓	Credit ✓
Petty cash control	56.01		✓
Distribution expenses	5.60	✓	
Office expenses	28.60	✓	
Travel	17.65	✓	
VAT	4.16	✓	

Task 1.5

(a) – (c)

Office expenses

Date 20XX	Details	Amount £	Date 20XX	Details	Amount £
01 Jun	Balance b/d	12,945			
30 Jun	Petty cash	42			
30 Jun	Purchases ledger control	523			
			30 Jun	Balance c/d	13,510
	Total	13,510		Total	13,510
1 Jul	Balance b/d	13,510			

Commission received

Date 20XX	Details	Amount £	Date 20XX	Details	Amount £
			01 Jun	Balance b/d	1,276
			30 Jun	Bank	18
30 Jun	Balance c/d	1,294			
	Total	1,294		Total	1,294
			1 Jul	Balance b/d	1,294

Task 1.6

Account name	Amount £	Debit £	Credit £
Advertising	789	789	
Bank overdraft	2,137		2,137
Capital	5,000		5,000
Commission income	1,356		1,356
Discounts allowed	1,986	1,986	
Discounts received	2,543		2,543
Distribution expenses	9,110	9,110	
Furniture and fittings	18,750	18,750	
Inventory	12,354	12,354	
Loan from bank	10,000		10,000
Maintenance	1,035	1,035	
Office expenses	13,728	13,728	
Petty cash	250	250	
Purchases	66,390	66,390	
Purchases ledger control	6,297		6,297
Purchases returns	3,287		3,287
Rent and rates	8,265	8,265	
Sales	172,242		172,242
Sales ledger control	24,910	24,910	
Sales returns	2,890	2,890	
Telephone and internet	2,165	2,165	
Travel	1,023	1,023	
VAT owing to HM Revenue & Customs	5,320		5,320
Wages and salaries	44,537	44,537	
Totals		208,182	208,182

Section 2

Task 2.1

(a) and (b)

Purchases returns day book

Date 20XX	Details	Credit note number	Total £	VAT £	Net £	Purchases returns £
30 Jun	Sindar Ltd	CN873	2,112	352	1,760	1,760
30 Jun	Premier Inc	02936	2,496	416	2,080	2,080
30 Jun	Bargain Parts plc	1092/22	144	24	120	120
	Totals		4,752	792	3,960	3,960

Task 2.2

VAT: $((5,000 \times 22/50) - (5,000 \times 22/50 \times 20/100)) \times 20/100 = 352$

Total: $(5,000 \times 22/50) \times 0.80 \times 1.2 = 2,112$

	Yes ✓	No ✓
Has the correct purchase price of the facings been charged?		✓
Has the correct discount rate been applied?	✓	
What would be the VAT amount charged if the invoice was correct?	£	352
What would be the total amount charged if the invoice was correct?	£	2,112

Task 2.3

(a)

Supplier code	F920
General ledger code	GL971

(b) The correct answer is: to help identify the amount spent on a particular category of inventory

Task 2.4

(a) The correct answer is: discount for £27

(b) The correct answer is: credit note C043

(c) The correct answer is: £9,696

Working

£9,723 – £27 = £9,696

....

Task 2.5

(a)

Hazelcombe & Co
42 Turnstile Trading Estate
Luscombe
LU9 0FG

REMITTANCE ADVICE

To: Cooper Foundry Ltd   Date: 27 July 20XX

Please find attached our cheque in payment of the following amounts.

Invoice number	Credit note number	Amount £
09528		2,386
	124	63
	Total amount paid	2,323

(b) The correct answer is: August

....

Task 2.6

(a) VAT: $(800 - (800 \times 2/100)) \times 20/100 = 156.80$

Hazelcombe & Co
42 Turnstile Trading Estate
Luscombe
LU9 0FG

VAT Registration No. 928 2781 110

Warriner plc   Customer account code: W981
45 Printer Lane
Luscombe
LU3 9LA

Date: 11 July 20XX

Invoice No: 21026
Delivery note number: 90230

Quantity of goods	Product code	Total list price £	Net amount after trade discount £	VAT £	Gross £
500	FX827	1,000.00	800.00	156.80	956.80

(b) The correct answer is: bulk discount

Task 2.7

Hazelcombe & Co
42 Turnstile Trading Estate
Luscombe
LU9 0FG

To: Tarsus & Co   Date: 31 July 20XX

Date 20XX	Details	Transaction amount £	Outstanding amount £
13 July	Invoice 21104	1,430	1,430
17 July	Credit note 920	213	1,217
22 July	Invoice 21309	947	2,164
30 July	Cheque	1,020	1,144
30 July	Discount taken	15	1,129

Task 2.8

(a) The correct answer is: sales invoice 21276

(b) The correct answer is: £1,387.68

Working

(£1,180 × 98%) + £231.28 = <u>£1,387.68</u>

(c) The correct answer is: £1,411.28

Working

(1,180.00 + 231.28 = 1,411.28)

Task 2.9

Item	Capital expenditure ✓	Revenue expenditure ✓	Capital income ✓	Revenue income ✓
Cash sales				✓
Purchase on credit of lights for resale		✓		
Sale of goods on credit				✓
Purchase of office computer	✓			
Payments to credit suppliers		✓		
Receipt from sale of an item of Hazelcombe & Co's furniture and fittings			✓	

Task 2.10

(a)

	True ✓	False ✓
An increase in an asset is shown as a credit entry in the general ledger		✓
A decrease in liabilities is shown as a credit entry in the general ledger		✓
An increase in capital is shown as a credit entry in the general ledger	✓	

(b)

Item	Example
Asset	Trade receivables
Liability	Bank overdraft
Capital transaction	Drawings

BPP PRACTICE ASSESSMENT 3
BASIC ACCOUNTING I

Time allowed: 2 hours

Basic Accounting I BPP practice assessment 3: Mandarin Ltd

Mandarin Ltd sells clothing for adults via two shops.

All answers should be rounded to the nearest penny unless otherwise instructed.

Section 1

Task 1.1

The following transactions all took place on 30 June and have been entered into the sales day book as shown below. No entries have yet been made into the ledger system.

Sales day book

Date 20XX	Details	Invoice number	Total £	VAT @ 20% £	Net £
30 Jun	Trencher plc	3452	672	112	560
30 Jun	Simons and Daughters	3453	1,968	328	1,640
30 Jun	Coker Ltd	3454	864	144	720
30 Jun	Marchmain & Co	3455	3,024	504	2,520
	Totals		6,528	1,088	5,440

(a) **What will be the entries in the sales ledger?**

Sales ledger

Account name	Amount £	Debit ✓	Credit ✓
▼			
▼			
▼			
▼			

Picklist:

Coker Ltd
Marchmain & Co
Purchases
Purchases ledger control
Purchases returns
Sales
Sales ledger control

Sales returns
Simons and Daughters
Trencher plc
VAT

(b) **What will be the entries in the general ledger?**

General ledger

Account name	Amount £	Debit ✓	Credit ✓
▼			
▼			
▼			

Picklist:

Coker Ltd
Marchmain & Co
Purchases
Purchases ledger control
Purchases returns
Sales
Sales ledger control
Sales returns
Simons and Daughters
Trencher plc
VAT

Task 1.2

The following credit transactions all took place on 30 June and have been entered into the purchases returns day book as shown below. No entries have yet been made in the ledgers.

Purchases returns day book

Date 20XX	Details	Credit note number	Total £	VAT £	Net £
30 June	Bester plc	0923	96	16	80
30 June	Newsome Ltd	C6478	432	72	360
	Totals		528	88	440

(a) **What will be the entries in the purchases ledger?**

Purchases ledger

Account name	Amount £	Debit ✓	Credit ✓
▼			
▼			

Picklist:

Bester plc
Newsome Ltd
Purchases
Purchases ledger control
Purchases returns
Sales
Sales ledger control
Sales returns
VAT

(b) **What will be the entries in the general ledger?**

General ledger

Account name	Amount £	Debit ✓	Credit ✓
▼			
▼			
▼			

Picklist:

Bester plc
Newsome Ltd
Purchases
Purchases ledger control
Purchases returns
Sales
Sales ledger control
Sales returns
VAT

Task 1.3

The following transactions all took place on 30 June and have been entered in the debit side of the cash book as shown below. No entries have yet been made in the ledgers.

Cash book – Debit side

Date 20XX	Details	VAT £	Bank £
30 Jun	Singer & Co		1,934
30 Jun	Cash sale	126	756
		126	2,690

(a) **What will be the entry in the sales ledger?**

Sales ledger

Account name	Amount £	Debit ✓	Credit ✓
▼			

Picklist:

Bank
Discounts allowed
Discounts received
Purchases
Purchases ledger control
Sales
Sales ledger control
Singer & Co
VAT

(b) **What will be the THREE entries in the general ledger?**

General ledger

Account name	Amount £	Debit ✓	Credit ✓
▼			
▼			
▼			

Picklist:

Bank
Discounts allowed
Discounts received
Purchases
Purchases ledger control

Sales
Sales ledger control
Singer & Co
VAT

The following transactions took place on 30 June and have been entered in the credit side of the cash book as shown below. No entries have yet been made in the ledgers.

Cash book – Credit side

Date 20XX	Details	Discount £	Bank £
30 Jun	Balance b/d		966
30 Jun	Vincent plc	121	2,377

(c) **What will be the THREE entries in the general ledger?**

General ledger

Account name	Amount £	Debit ✓	Credit ✓
▼			
▼			
▼			

Picklist:

Bank
Discounts allowed
Discounts received
Purchases
Purchases ledger control
Sales
Sales ledger control
VAT
Vincent plc

Task 1.4

Mandarin Ltd maintains a petty cash book as a book of prime entry only. The following transactions all took place on 30 June and have been entered in the petty cash book (credit side) as shown below. No entries have yet been made in the general ledger.

Petty cash book – Credit side

Date 20XX	Details	Amount £	VAT @ 20% £	Motor expenses £	Postage £	Sundry expenses £
30 Jun	Taxi fares	15.98				15.98
30 Jun	Printer paper	8.16	1.36			6.80
30 Jun	Petrol	51.36	8.56	42.80		
30 Jun	Postage stamps	17.26			17.26	
		92.76	9.92	42.80	17.26	22.78

What will be the FIVE entries in the general ledger?

General ledger

Account name	Amount £	Debit ✓	Credit ✓
▼			
▼			
▼			
▼			
▼			

Picklist:

Bank
Motor expenses
Sundry expenses
Petrol
Petty cash control
Postage
Postage stamps
Printer paper
Taxi fares
VAT

Task 1.5

The following two accounts are in the general ledger at the close of day on 30 June.

(a) **Insert the balance carried down together with date and details.**
(b) **Insert the totals.**
(c) **Insert the balance brought down together with date and details.**

Motor expenses

Date 20XX	Details	Amount £	Date 20XX	Details	Amount £
01 Jun	Balance b/d	2,904		▼	
15 Jun	Purchases ledger control	276		▼	
30 Jun	Purchases ledger control	184		▼	
	▼			▼	
	Total			Total	
	▼			▼	

Picklist:

Balance b/d
Balance c/d
Bank
Purchases ledger control
Sales ledger control

Discounts received

Date 20XX	Details	Amount £	Date 20XX	Details	Amount £
	▼		01 Jun	Balance b/d	926
	▼		15 Jun	Purchases ledger control	64
	▼		30 Jun	Purchases ledger control	25
	▼			▼	
	Total			Total	
	▼			▼	

Picklist:

Balance b/d
Balance c/d
Bank
Purchases ledger control
Sales ledger control

Task 1.6

Below is a list of balances to be transferred to the trial balance as at 30 June.

Place the figures in the debit or credit column, as appropriate, and total each column.

Account name	Amount £	Debit £	Credit £
Marketing	2,534		
Cash at bank	9,267		
Capital	10,000		
Heat and light	3,289		
Discounts allowed	1,004		
Discounts received	2,940		
Motor expenses	3,098		
Motor vehicles	15,000		
Loan from bank	12,500		
Administration expenses	5,903		
Insurance	498		
Petty cash	100		
Purchases	89,262		
Purchases ledger control	7,438		
Purchases returns	2,907		
Premises costs	5,097		
Sales	166,242		
Sales ledger control	11,892		
Sales returns	3,022		
Inventory	16,006		
Training expenses	2,786		
Travel	457		
VAT owing to HM Revenue & Customs	2,455		
Salaries	35,267		
Totals			

Section 2

Task 2.1

Invoices from suppliers have been checked and partially entered in the purchases day book, as shown below.

(a) **Complete the entries in the purchases day book by inserting the appropriate figures for each invoice.**

(b) **Total the last five columns of the purchases day book.**

Purchases day book

Date 20XX	Details	Invoice number	Total £	VAT @ 20% £	Net £	Women's clothing £	Men's clothing £
30 Jun	Forfar Textiles plc	C9230	1,872				1,560
30 Jun	Jessamy Fashion Inc	0024567	3,216		2,680	2,680	
30 Jun	Lindstrom Ltd	726		648		3,240	
	Totals						

Task 2.2

A supply of clothing has been delivered to Mandarin Ltd by Rainbow Fashions Ltd. The purchase order sent from Mandarin Ltd, and the invoice from Rainbow Fashions Ltd, are shown below.

Mandarin Ltd
Mandarin House, 25 Jedward Street
Cinnadon
CN6 6LW

Purchase Order No. 093247

To: Rainbow Fashions Ltd

Date: 17 July 20XX

Please supply 40 mens polo shirts, product code MPS45
Purchase price: £36 00 per pack of 5, plus VAT
Discount: less 10% trade discount, as agreed.

Rainbow Fashions Ltd
92 Norman Street, Cinnadon CN4 2KJ
VAT Registration No. 903 2838 39

Invoice No. 83792

Mandarin Ltd
Mandarin House, 25 Jedward Street
Cinnadon
CN6 6LW

22 July 20XX

40 mens polo shirts product code MPS45 @ £7.60 each	£304.00
Less: trade discount at 10%	£30.40
Net amount	£273.60
VAT @ 20%	£54.72
Total	£328.32

Terms: 30 days net

Check the invoice against the purchase order and answer the following questions.

	Yes ✓	No ✓
Has the correct purchase price of the polo shirts been charged?		
Has the correct discount been applied?		
What would be the VAT amount charged if the invoice was correct?	£	
What would be the total amount charged if the invoice was correct?	£	

Task 2.3

Mandarin Ltd codes all purchase invoices with a supplier code AND a general ledger code. A selection of the codes used is given below.

Supplier	Supplier Code
Dapple Ltd	PL189
Gadabout UK plc	PL394
Indigo & Co	PL522
New Aim Ltd	PL703
Roughtrap Ltd	PL947

Item	General Ledger Code
Men's shirts	GL001
Men's trousers	GL002
Women's tops	GL003
Women's trousers	GL004
Sundry clothing	GL005

This is an invoice received from a supplier.

New Aim Ltd
35 Didcot Road, Cinnadon CN7 3DD
VAT Registration No. 356 2368 302

Mandarin Ltd
Mandarin House
25 Jedward Street
Cinnadon
CN6 6LW

23 July 20XX

30 womens trousers (product code WT673) @ £16 each	£480.00
VAT @ 20%	£96.00
Total	£576.00

(a) **Select which codes would be used to code this invoice.**

Supplier code	▼
General ledger code	▼

Picklist:

GL001
GL002
GL003
GL004
GL005
PL189
PL394
PL522
PL703
PL947

(b) In order to identify how much is owed to a supplier at any point in time, purchases invoices are coded with a

Picklist:

General ledger code
Supplier code
Customer code
Product code

Task 2.4

Shown below is a statement of account received from a credit supplier, and the supplier's account as shown in the purchases ledger of Mandarin Ltd.

Bella Designs
34-36 Bath Street
Cinnadon
CN3 1GH

To: Mandarin Ltd
Mandarin House
25 Jedward Street
Cinnadon
CN6 6LW

STATEMENT OF ACCOUNT

Date 20XX	Number	Details	Amount £	Balance £
26 May	6723	Invoice	1,092	1,092
3 June	6801	Invoice	894	1,986
15 June		Payment	–1,986	0
15 June	7013	Invoice	3,267	3,267
18 June	C67	Credit note	–62	3,205
27 Jun	7226	Invoice	2,674	5,879
30 June	C98	Credit note	–89	5,790

Bella Designs

Date 20XX	Details	Amount £	Date 20XX	Details	Amount £
15 June	Bank – cheque	1,986	26 May	Purchases	1,092
18 June	Purchases returns	62	3 June	Purchases	894
30 June	Bank – cheque	3,205	15 June	Purchases	3,267
			27 June	Purchases	2,674

(a) **Which item is missing from the statement of account from Bella Designs?**

▼

Picklist:

Credit note C67
Credit note C98
Invoice 6723
Invoice 6801
Invoice 7013
Invoice 7226
Payment for £1,986
Payment for £3,205

(b) **Which item is missing from the supplier account in Mandarin Ltd's purchases ledger?**

▼

Picklist:

Credit note C67
Credit note C98
Invoice 6723
Invoice 6801
Invoice 7013
Invoice 7226
Payment for £1,986
Payment for £3,205

(c) **Assuming any differences between the statement of account from Bella Designs and the supplier account in Mandarin Ltd's purchases ledger are simply due to omission errors, what is the amount owing to Bella Designs?**

£ [   ]

Task 2.5

Mandarin Ltd sends out cheques to suppliers on the last working day of the month following the month of the relevant invoice or credit note. Below is an extract from the purchases ledger of Mandarin Ltd.

Lena Couture plc

Date 20XX	Details	Amount £	Date 20XX	Details	Amount £
22 May	Purchases returns (credit note 22)	72	19 May	Purchases invoice 6738	675
21 June	Purchases returns (credit note 25)	141	16 June	Purchases Invoice 6759	1,926
30 June	Bank	603	24 July	Purchases Invoice 6925	2,007

(a) **Complete the remittance advice note for Mandarin Ltd's payment to the supplier on 31 July 20XX, the last working day of July.**

Mandarin Ltd
Mandarin House
25 Jedward Street
Cinnadon
CN6 6LW

REMITTANCE ADVICE

To: Lena Couture plc   Date: 31 July 20XX

Please find attached our cheque in payment of the following amounts.

Invoice number	Credit note number	Amount £
	Total amount paid	

(b) **Which of the following statements is True?**

	✓
The remittance advice note is a book of prime entry	
The remittance advice note is part of the general ledger	
The remittance advice note is part of the purchases ledger	
The remittance advice note is sent to the supplier	

Task 2.6

On 21 July Mandarin Ltd delivered the following goods to a credit customer, Jessop Brothers.

Mandarin Ltd
Mandarin House
25 Jedward Street
Cinnadon
CN6 6LW

Delivery note No. 452634
21 July 20XX

Jessop Brothers   Customer account code: SL930
Unit 10 Eastern Trading Estate
Cinnadon
CN1 1PP

720 womens decorative tops, product code WT555.

The list price of the goods was £30 per box of 6 tops plus VAT. Jessop Brothers is to be given a 10% bulk discount and a 5% early settlement discount.

(a) **Complete the invoice below.**

Mandarin Ltd
Mandarin House, 25 Jedward Street
Cinnadon
CN6 6LW

VAT Registration No. 928 2781 110

Jessop Brothers   Customer account code: SL930
Unit 10 Eastern Trading Estate
Cinnadon
CN1 1PP

   Date: 22 July 20XX
Invoice No:01256
Delivery note number: 452634

Quantity of goods	Product code	Total list price £	Net amount after bulk discount £	VAT £	Gross £

Mandarin Ltd offers some established customers a discount of 5% whatever the size of their order and irrespective of when they pay.

(b) **What is the name of this type of discount?**

▼

Picklist:

Bulk discount
Settlement discount
Trade discount

Task 2.7

The following is a summary of transactions with Tarsus & Co, a new credit customer.

£324 re invoice 01250 of 21 July
£12 re credit note 013 of 22 July
£1,285 re invoice 01301 of 30 July
Cheque for £302 received 31 July
Settlement discount £10 taken 31 July

Complete the statement of account below.

Mandarin Ltd
Mandarin House
25 Jedward Street
Cinnadon
CN6 6LW

To: Tarsus & Co   Date: 31 July 20XX

Date 20XX	Details	Transaction amount £	Outstanding amount £
21 July	Invoice 01250		
22 July	Credit note 013		
30 July	Invoice 01301		
31 July	Cheque		
31 July	Discount taken		

Task 2.8

The account shown below is in the sales ledger of Mandarin Ltd. A remittance advice for an automated payment of £1,565 has now been received from this customer.

Plews & Co

Date 20XX	Details	Amount £	Date 20XX	Details	Amount £
12 May	Sales invoice 0024	2,910	15 May	Sales returns credit note 001	125
23 June	Sales invoice 0095	1,663	25 June	Sales returns credit note 017	98
2 July	Sales invoice 0102	2,739	30 June	Bank	2,785

(a) **Which outstanding item has not been included in the payment of £1,565?**

Picklist:

Sales invoice 0024
Sales invoice 0095
Sales invoice 0102
Bank
Sales returns credit note 001
Sales returns credit note 017

An invoice is being prepared to be sent to Plews & Co for £2,560.00 plus VAT of £486.40. A settlement discount of 5% will be offered for payment within 10 days.

(b) **What is the amount Mandarin Ltd should receive if payment is made within 10 days?**

£ [   ]

(c) **What is the amount Mandarin Ltd should receive if payment is NOT made within 10 days?**

£ [   ]

Task 2.9

It is important to understand the difference between capital expenditure, revenue expenditure, capital income and revenue income.

Select one option in each instance below to show whether the item will be capital expenditure, revenue expenditure, capital income or revenue income.

Item	Capital expenditure ✓	Revenue expenditure ✓	Capital income ✓	Revenue income ✓
Receipt from sale of a motor vehicle				
Purchase on credit of clothing for resale				
Sale of clothing with one month to pay				
Purchase of shop fittings				
Sale in the factory shop with payment by debit card				
Payment to supplier with one month credit taken				

Task 2.10

(a) **Show whether the following statements are True or False.**

	True ✓	False ✓
In a cash transaction the primary documentation is a (till) receipt		
Output tax is the VAT suffered on purchases		
Every three months every business must pay value added tax to HMRC		

(b) **For each of the items below, identify an example from the picklist provided.**

Item	Example	
Asset		▼
Liability		▼
Capital transaction		▼

Picklist:

Trade payables
Contribution from owners
Petty cash

BPP PRACTICE ASSESSMENT 3
BASIC ACCOUNTING I

ANSWERS

Basic Accounting I BPP practice assessment 3: Mandarin Ltd

Section 1

Task 1.1

The following transactions

(a)

Sales ledger

Account name	Amount £	Debit ✓	Credit ✓
Trencher plc	672	✓	
Simons and Daughters	1,968	✓	
Coker Ltd	864	✓	
Marchmain & Co	3,024	✓	

(b)

General ledger

Account name	Amount £	Debit ✓	Credit ✓
Sales	5,440		✓
Sales ledger control	6,528	✓	
VAT	1,088		✓

Task 1.2

(a)

Purchases ledger

Account name	Amount £	Debit ✓	Credit ✓
Bester plc	96	✓	
Newsome Ltd	432	✓	

(b)

General ledger

Account name	Amount £	Debit ✓	Credit ✓
Purchases ledger control	528	✓	
Purchases returns	440		✓
VAT	88		✓

Task 1.3

(a)

Sales ledger

Account name	Amount £	Debit ✓	Credit ✓
Singer & Co	1,934		✓

(b)

General ledger

Account name	Amount £	Debit ✓	Credit ✓
Sales ledger control	1,934		✓
Sales	630		✓
VAT	126		✓

(c)

Purchases ledger

Account name	Amount £	Debit ✓	Credit ✓
Purchases ledger control	2,377	✓	
Purchases ledger control	121	✓	
Discount received	121		✓

Task 1.4

General ledger

Account name	Amount £	Debit ✓	Credit ✓
Petty cash control	92.76		✓
Motor expenses	42.80	✓	
Sundry expenses	22.78	✓	
Postage	17.26	✓	
VAT	9.92	✓	

Task 1.5

(a) – (c)

Motor expenses

Date 20XX	Details	Amount £	Date 20XX	Details	Amount £
01 Jun	Balance b/d	2,904			
15 Jun	Purchases ledger control	276			
30 Jun	Purchases ledger control	184			
			30 Jun	Balance c/d	3,364
	Total	3,364		Total	3,364
1 Jul	Balance b/d	3,364			

Discounts received

Date 20XX	Details	Amount £	Date 20XX	Details	Amount £
			01 Jun	Balance b/d	926
			15 Jun	PLCA	64
			30 Jun	PLCA	25
30 Jun	Balance c/d	1,015			
	Total	1,015		Total	1,015
			1 Jul	Balance b/d	1,015

Task 1.6

Account name	Amount £	Debit £	Credit £
Marketing	2,534	2,534	
Cash at bank	9,267	9,267	
Capital	10,000		10,000
Heat and light	3,289	3,289	
Discounts allowed	1,004	1,004	
Discounts received	2,940		2,940
Motor expenses	3,098	3,098	
Motor vehicles	15,000	15,000	
Loan from bank	12,500		12,500
Administration expenses	5,903	5,903	
Insurance	498	498	
Petty cash	100	100	
Purchases	89,262	89,262	
Purchases ledger control	7,438		7,438
Purchases returns	2,907		2,907
Premises costs	5,097	5,097	
Sales	166,242		166,242
Sales ledger control	11,892	11,892	
Sales returns	3,022	3,022	
Inventory	16,006	16,006	
Training expenses	2,786	2,786	
Travel	457	457	
VAT owing to HM Revenue & Customs	2,455		2,455
Salaries	35,267	35,267	
Totals		204,482	204,482

Section 2

Task 2.1

(a) – (b)

Purchases day book

Date 20XX	Details	Invoice number	Total £	VAT £	Net £	Women's clothing £	Men's clothing £
30 Jun	Forfar Textiles plc	C9230	1,872	312	1,560		1,560
30 Jun	Jessamy Fashion Inc	0024567	3,216	536	2,680	2,680	
30 Jun	Lindstrom Ltd	726	3,888	648	3,240	3,240	
	Totals		8,976	1,496	7,480	5,920	1,560

Task 2.2

VAT: $((40 \times 36/5) - (40 \times 36/5 \times 10/100)) \times 20/100 = 51.84$

Total: $((40 \times 36/5) - (40 \times 36/5 \times 10/100)) \times 120/100 = 311.04$

	Yes ✓	No ✓
Has the correct purchase price of the polo shirts been charged?		✓
Has the correct discount been applied?	✓	
What would be the VAT amount charged if the invoice was correct?	£	51.84
What would be the total amount charged if the invoice was correct?	£	311.04

Task 2.3

(a)

Supplier code	PL703
General ledger code	GL004

(b)   The correct answer is: supplier code

Task 2.4

(a)   The correct answer is: payment for £3,205

(b)   The correct answer is: credit note C98

(c)   The correct answer is: £2,585

Working

£5,790 – £3,205 = <u>£2,585</u>

Task 2.5

(a)

Mandarin Ltd
Mandarin House
25 Jedward Street
Cinnadon
CN6 6LW

REMITTANCE ADVICE

To: Lena Couture plc	Date: 31 July 20XX

Please find attached our cheque in payment of the following amounts.

Invoice number	Credit note number	Amount £
6759		1,926
	25	141
	Total amount paid	1,785

(b)   The correct answer is: the remittance advice note is sent to the supplier

Task 2.6

(a)

Mandarin Ltd
Mandarin House, 25 Jedward Street
Cinnadon
CN6 6LW

VAT Registration No. 928 2781 110

Jessop Brothers	Customer account code: SL930
Unit 10 Eastern Trading Estate	
Cinnadon	
CN1 1PP	

Invoice No:01256	Date: 22 July 20XX
Delivery note number: 452634	

Quantity of goods	Product code	Total list price £	Net amount after bulk discount £	VAT £	Gross £
720	WT555	3,600.00	3,240.00	615.60	3,855.60

(b) The correct answer is: trade discount

Task 2.7

Mandarin Ltd
Mandarin House
25 Jedward Street
Cinnadon
CN6 6LW

To: Tarsus & Co	Date: 31 July 20XX

Date 20XX	Details	Transaction amount £	Outstanding amount £
21 July	Invoice 01250	324	324
22 July	Credit note 013	−12	312
30 July	Invoice 01301	1,285	1,597
31 July	Cheque	−302	1,295
31 July	Discount taken	−10	1,285

Task 2.8

(a) The correct answer is: sales invoice 0102

(b) The correct answer is: £2,918.40

Working

(£2,560.00 × 95%) + £486.40 = £2,918.40

(c) The correct answer is: £3,046.40

Working

£2,560.00 + £486.40 = £3,046.40

Task 2.9

Item	Capital expenditure ✓	Revenue expenditure ✓	Capital income ✓	Revenue income ✓
Receipt from sale of a motor vehicle			✓	
Purchase on credit of clothing for resale		✓		
Sale of clothing with one month to pay				✓
Purchase of shop fittings	✓			
Sale in the factory shop with payment by debit card				✓
Payment to suppliers with one month credit taken		✓		

Task 2.10

(a)

	True ✓	False ✓
In a cash transaction the primary documentation is a (till) receipt	✓	
Output tax is the VAT suffered on purchases		✓
Every three months every business must pay value added tax (VAT) to HMRC		✓

(b)

Item	Example
Asset	Petty cash
Liability	Trade payables
Capital transaction	Contribution from owners

BPP PRACTICE ASSESSMENT 4
BASIC ACCOUNTING I

Time allowed: 2 hours

Basic Accounting I BPP practice assessment 4: Sumberton Ltd

Sumberton Ltd sells bags and suitcases to shops.

All answers should be rounded to the nearest penny unless otherwise instructed.

Section 1

Task 1.1

The following transactions all took place on 30 November and have been entered into the sales day book as shown below. No entries have yet been made into the ledger system.

Sales day book

Date 20XX	Details	Invoice number	Total £	VAT @ 20% £	Net £
30 Nov	Gringles Co	12786	300	50	250
30 Nov	Lester plc	12787	1,308	218	1,090
30 Nov	Shrier Goods	12788	2,676	446	2,230
30 Nov	Abunda Bags	12789	1,992	332	1,660
	Totals		6,276	1,046	5,230

(a) **What will be the entries in the sales ledger?**

Sales ledger

Account name	Amount £	Debit ✓	Credit ✓
▼			
▼			
▼			

Picklist:

Abunda Bags
Gringles Co
Lester plc
Purchases
Purchases ledger control
Purchases returns
Sales
Sales ledger control
Sales returns
Shrier Goods
VAT

(b) **What will be the entries in the general ledger?**

General ledger

Account name	Amount £	Debit ✓	Credit ✓
▼			
▼			
▼			

Picklist:

Abunda Bags
Gringles Co
Lester plc
Purchases
Purchases ledger control
Purchases returns
Sales
Sales ledger control
Sales returns
Shrier Goods
VAT

Task 1.2

The following credit transactions all took place on 30 November and have been entered into the purchases day book as shown below. No entries have yet been made in the ledgers.

Purchases day book

Date 20XX	Details	Invoice number	Total £	VAT @ 20% £	Net £
30 Nov	Frankie's Leatherware	0923	12,348	2,058	10,290
30 Nov	Casaubon's	C6478	3,924	654	3,270
	Totals		16,272	2,712	13,560

(a) **What will be the entries in the purchases ledger?**

Purchases ledger

Account name	Amount £	Debit ✓	Credit ✓
▼			
▼			

Picklist:

Casaubon's
Frankie's Leatherware
Purchases
Purchases ledger control
Purchases returns
Sales
Sales ledger control
Sales returns
VAT

(b) **What will be the entries in the general ledger?**

General ledger

Account name	Amount £	Debit ✓	Credit ✓
▼			
▼			
▼			

Picklist:

Casaubon's
Frankie's Leatherware
Purchases
Purchases ledger control
Purchases returns
Sales
Sales ledger control
Sales returns
VAT

Task 1.3

The following transactions all took place on 30 November and have been entered in the credit side of the cash book as shown below. No entries have yet been made in the ledgers.

Cash book – Credit side

Date 20XX	Details	VAT @ 20% £	Bank £
30 Nov	Cash purchase	102	612
30 Nov	Casaubon's		2,445

(a) **What will be the entry in the purchases ledger?**

Purchases ledger

Account name	Amount £	Debit ✓	Credit ✓
▼			

Picklist:

Bank
Casaubon's
Discounts allowed
Discounts received
Purchases
Purchases ledger control
Sales
Sales ledger control
VAT

(b) **What will be the THREE entries in the general ledger?**

General ledger

Account name	Amount £	Debit ✓	Credit ✓
▼			
▼			
▼			

Picklist:

Bank
Casaubon's
Discounts allowed
Discounts received
Purchases
Purchases ledger control
Sales
Sales ledger control
VAT

The following transactions took place on 30 November and have been entered in the debit side of the cash book as shown below. No entries have yet been made in the ledgers.

Cash book – Debit side

Date 20XX	Details	Discount £	Bank £
30 Nov	Balance b/d		3,208
30 Nov	Abunda Bags	56	3,984

(c) **What will be the THREE entries in the general ledger?**

General ledger

Account name	Amount £	Debit ✓	Credit ✓
▼			
▼			
▼			

Picklist:

Abunda Bags
Bank
Discounts allowed
Discounts received
Purchases
Purchases ledger control
Sales
Sales ledger control
VAT

Task 1.4

Sumberton Ltd maintains a petty cash book as both a book of prime entry and a general ledger account. The following transactions all took place on 30 November and have been entered in the credit side of the petty cash book as shown below. No entries have yet been made in the general ledger.

Petty cash book – Credit side

Date 20XX	Details £	Amount £	VAT @ 20% £	Office expenses £	Travel £	Purchases £
30 Nov	Bag for resale	24.00	4.00			20.00
30 Nov	Envelopes	18.24	3.04	15.20		
30 Nov	Bus ticket	27.00			27.00	
30 Nov	Postage stamps	22.60		22.60		
		91.84	7.04	37.80	27.00	20.00

(a) **What will be the FOUR entries in the general ledger?**

General ledger

Account name	Amount £	Debit ✓	Credit ✓
▼			
▼			
▼			
▼			

Picklist:

Bag for resale
Bank
Bus ticket
Envelopes
Office expenses
Petty cash control
Postage stamps
Purchases
Travel
VAT

(b) Sumberton Ltd started the day on 30 November with a £200 imprest.

What amount must be withdrawn from the bank and placed in the petty cash box in order to restore the imprest at the end of the day?

£

Task 1.5

The following two accounts are in the general ledger at the close of day on 30 November.

(a) **Insert the balance carried down together with date and details.**
(b) **Insert the totals.**
(c) **Insert the balance brought down together with date and details.**

Purchases

Date 20XX	Details	Amount £	Date 20XX	Details	Amount £
01 Nov	Balance b/d	140,389		▼	
15 Nov	Purchases ledger control	14,388		▼	
30 Nov	Purchases ledger control	52,389		▼	
		▼		▼	
	Total			Total	
		▼		▼	

Picklist:

Balance b/d
Balance c/d
Bank
Purchases
Purchases ledger control
Sales ledger control

Bank interest received

Date 20XX	Details	Amount £	Date 20XX	Details	Amount £
	▼		01 Nov	Balance b/d	32
	▼		15 Nov	Bank	14
	▼		30 Nov	Bank	22
	▼			▼	
	Total			Total	
	▼			▼	

Picklist:

Balance b/d
Balance c/d
Bank
Bank interest received
Purchases ledger control
Sales ledger control

Task 1.6

Below is a list of balances to be transferred to the trial balance as at 30 November.

Place the figures in the debit or credit column, as appropriate, and total each column.

Account name	Amount £	Debit £	Credit £
Maintenance expenses	6,082		
Cash at bank	22,241		
Capital	24,000		
Heat and light	7,893		
Discounts allowed	2,409		
Discounts received	7,056		
Motor expenses	7,435		
Machinery	36,000		
Computer equipment	8,018		
Sundry expenses	14,167		
Legal expenses	1,195		
Office expenses	1,221		
Petty cash	200		
Purchases	214,229		
Purchases ledger control	17,851		
Rent and rates	6,976		
Sales	421,956		
Sales ledger control	28,540		
Sales returns	7,252		
Inventory	38,414		
Bank interest received	1,253		
Travel	1,096		
VAT owing to HM Revenue & Customs	15,892		
Salaries	84,640		
Totals			

Section 2

Task 2.1

Credit notes to customers have been prepared and partially entered in the sales returns day book, as shown below.

(a) **Complete the entries in the sales returns day book by inserting the appropriate figures for each credit note.**

(b) **Total the last five columns of the sales returns day book.**

Sales returns day book

Date 20XX	Details	Credit note number	Total £	VAT @ 20% £	Net £	Bags returns £	Suitcases returns £
30 Nov	Shrier Goods	562		104		520	
30 Nov	Gringles Co	563	408				340
30 Nov	Lester plc	564	1,068		890	890	
	Totals						

Task 2.2

A supply of suitcases has been delivered to Sumberton Ltd by Casaubon's. The purchase order sent from Sumberton Ltd, and the invoice from Casaubon's, are shown below.

Sumberton Ltd
Sumberton House, 10 Main Road
Sawlow
SA7 5LD

Purchase Order No. 7683247

To: Casaubon's

Date: 17 December 20XX

Please supply 15 small wheeled cabin cases, product code WCC625
Purchase price: £23 each, plus VAT
Discount: less 15% trade discount, as agreed.

Casaubon's
80 Eliot Street, Sawlow SA9 4AC
VAT Registration No. 983 3933 83

Invoice No. 782736

Sumberton Ltd
Sumberton House, 10 Main Road
Sawlow
SA7 5LD

22 December 20XX

15 small wheeled cabin cases product code WCC625 @ £25 each	£375.00
Less: trade discount at 5%	£18.75
Net amount	£356.25
VAT @ 20%	£71.25
Total	£427.50

Terms: 30 days net

Check the invoice against the purchase order and answer the following questions.

	Yes ✓	No ✓
Has the correct purchase price of the cabin cases been charged?		
Has the correct discount been applied?		
What would be the VAT amount charged if the invoice was correct?	£	
What would be the total amount charged if the invoice was correct?	£	

Task 2.3

Sumberton Ltd codes all purchase invoices with a supplier code AND a general ledger code. A selection of the codes used is given below.

Supplier	Supplier Code
Casaubon's	PL012
Frankie's Leatherware	PL128
Jane Peel Ltd	PL244
Trinder and Papp	PL301
Wishburton Ltd	PL666

Item	General Ledger Code
Leather bags	GL001
Canvass bags	GL002
Wheeled cases	GL003
Carry cases	GL004
accessories	GL005

This is an invoice received from a supplier.

Jane Peel Ltd
56 Ward End Road, Doristown DO9 3YU
VAT Registration No. 134 1452 22

Sumberton Ltd
Sumberton House
10 Main Road
Sawlow
SA7 5LD

23 December 20XX

10 leather bags (product code R245L) @ £17.50 each	£175.00
VAT @ 20%	£35.00
Total	£210.00

(a) **Select which codes would be used to code this invoice.**

Supplier code	▼
General ledger code	▼

Picklist:

GL001
GL002
GL003
GL004
GL005
PL012
PL128
PL244
PL301
PL666

(b) In order to identify how much has been spent on a particular product for resale at any point in time, purchases invoices are coded with a

	▼

Picklist:

General ledger code
Supplier code
Customer code
Product code

Task 2.4

Shown below is a statement of account received from a credit supplier, and the supplier's account as shown in the purchases ledger of Sumberton Ltd.

Trinder and Papp
54 Vallais Road
Gosfirth
GO9 5VV

To: Sumberton Ltd
Sumberton House
10 Main Road
Sawlow
SA7 5LD

STATEMENT OF ACCOUNT

Date 20XX	Number	Details	Amount £	Balance £
20 October	10923	Invoice	2,109	2,109
4 November		Payment	−2,099	10
8 November	11004	Invoice	3,188	3,198
10 November	C536	Credit note	−156	3,042
26 November	11342	Invoice	2,185	5,227
28 November	11378	Invoice	1,244	6,471
30 November	C579	Credit note	−320	6,151

BPP
LEARNING MEDIA

Trinder and Papp

Date 20XX	Details	Amount £	Date 20XX	Details	Amount £
4 Nov	Bank – BACS	2,099	20 Oct	Purchases	2,109
4 Nov	Discount	10	8 Nov	Purchases	3,188
10 Nov	Purchases returns	156	26 Nov	Purchases	2,185
			28 Nov	Purchases	1,244

(a) **Which item is missing from the statement of account from Trinder and Papp?**

▼

Picklist:

Credit note C536
Credit note C579
Discount of £10
Invoice 10923
Invoice 11004
Invoice 11342
Invoice 11378
Payment for £2,099

(b) **Which item is missing from the supplier account in Sumberton Ltd's purchases ledger?**

▼

Picklist:

Credit note C536
Credit note C579
Discount of £10
Invoice 10923
Invoice 11004
Invoice 11342
Invoice 11378
Payment for £2,099

(c) **Assuming any differences between the statement of account from Trinder and Papp and the supplier account in Sumberton Ltd's purchases ledger are simply due to omission errors, what is the amount owing to Trinder and Papp?**

£

Task 2.5

Sumberton Ltd sends out cheques to suppliers on the last working day of the month following the month of the relevant invoice or credit note. Below is an extract from the purchases ledger of Sumberton Ltd.

Frankie's Leatherware

Date 20XX	Details	Amount £	Date 20XX	Details	Amount £
19 Oct	Purchases returns (credit note 120)	155	15 Oct	Purchases invoice 29104	2,173
25 Nov	Purchases returns (credit note 176)	337	22 Nov	Purchases Invoice 29333	3,222
30 Nov	Bank	2,018	17 Dec	Purchases Invoice 29782	1,834

(a) **Complete the remittance advice note for Sumberton Ltd's payment to the supplier on 31 December 20XX, the last working day of December.**

Sumberton Ltd
Sumberton House
10 Main Road
Sawlow
SA7 5LD

REMITTANCE ADVICE

To: Frankie's Leatherware   Date: 31 December 20XX

Please find attached our cheque in payment of the following amounts.

Invoice number	Credit note number	Amount £
	Total amount paid	

(b) **Which of the following statements is True?**

	✓
A credit note adds to the amount owed to the supplier	
A remittance advice note adds to the amount owed to the supplier	
A goods received note adds to the amount owed to the supplier	
An invoice adds to the amount owed to the supplier	

Task 2.6

On 21 December Sumberton Ltd delivered the following goods to a credit customer, Gringles Co.

Sumberton Ltd Sumberton House 10 Main Road Sawlow SA7 5LD

Delivery note No. 6734527
21 December 20XX

Gringles Co   Customer account code: SL637
Unit 18 Radley Estate
Sawlow
SA7 7VB

80 leather shoulder bags, product code L736B.

The list price of the goods was £100 per box of 5 bags plus VAT. Gringles Co is to be given a 15% bulk discount and a 4% discount if the invoice is paid within 10 days.

(a) **Complete the invoice below.**

Sumberton Ltd
Sumberton House,
10 Main Road
Sawlow
SA7 5LD

VAT Registration No. 536 3723 77

Gringles Co   Customer account code: SL637
Unit 18 Radley Estate
Sawlow
SA7 7VB

Date: 22 December 20XX

Invoice No:12901
Delivery note number: 6734527

Quantity of goods	Product code	Total list price £	Net amount after bulk discount £	VAT £	Gross £

Sumberton Ltd offers some established customers a discount of 4% whatever the size of their order and irrespective of when they pay.

(b) **What is the name of this type of discount?**

▼

Picklist:

Bulk discount
Settlement discount
Trade discount

....

Task 2.7

The following is a summary of transactions with Diamond Bags, a new credit customer.

£1,902 re invoice 12905 of 10 December
£219 re credit note 701 of 12 December
£733 re invoice 12916 of 30 December
Cheque for £1,668 received 31 December
Settlement discount £15 taken 31 December

Complete the statement of account below.

Sumberton Ltd
Sumberton House
10 Main Road
Sawlow
SA7 5LD

To: Diamond Bags   Date: 31 December 20XX

Date 20XX	Details	Transaction amount £	Outstanding amount £
10 December	Invoice 12905		
12 December	Credit note 701		
30 December	Invoice 12916		
31 December	Cheque		
31 December	Discount taken		

Task 2.8

The account shown below is in the sales ledger of Sumberton Ltd. A remittance advice for an automated payment of £2,807 has now been received from this customer.

Meering Ltd

Date 20XX	Details	Amount £	Date 20XX	Details	Amount £
6 October	Sales invoice 12624	1,756	10 October	Sales returns credit note 501	78
11 November	Sales invoice 12711	2,918	17 November	Sales returns credit note 555	111
7 December	Sales invoice 12813	2,384	30 November	Bank	1,678

(a) **Which outstanding item has not been included in the payment of £2,807?**

▼

Picklist:

Sales invoice 12624
Sales invoice 12711

Sales invoice 12813
Bank
Sales returns credit note 501
Sales returns credit note 555

An invoice is being prepared to be sent to Meering Ltd for £2,000 plus VAT of £384. A settlement discount of 4% will be offered for payment within 10 days.

(b) **What is the amount Sumberton Ltd should receive if payment is made within 10 days?**

£ [ ]

(c) **What is the amount Sumberton Ltd should receive if payment is NOT made within 10 days?**

£ [ ]

Task 2.9

It is important to understand the difference between capital expenditure, revenue expenditure, capital income and revenue income.

Select one option in each instance below to show whether the item will be capital expenditure, revenue expenditure, capital income or revenue income.

Item	Capital expenditure ✓	Revenue expenditure ✓	Capital income ✓	Revenue income ✓
Payment in advance for 3 months of phone line rental				
Proceeds from sale of machinery				
Sale of suitcases for cash				
Receipt of payment from trade receivable for bags				
Purchase of a shop building				
Petty cash payment for stationery				

Task 2.10

(a) **Show whether the following statements are True or False.**

	True ✓	False ✓
The book of original entry for discounts allowed is the petty cash book		
Input tax is the VAT suffered on purchases		
A goods received note is a primary document for recording in the accounting records		

(b) **For each of the items below, identify an example from the picklist provided.**

Item	Example
Asset	
Liability	
Capital transaction	

Picklist:

Drawings
Trade receivables
Bank overdraft

BPP PRACTICE ASSESSMENT 4
BASIC ACCOUNTING I

ANSWERS

Basic Accounting I BPP practice assessment 4: Sumberton Ltd

Section 1

Task 1.1

(a)

Sales ledger

Account name	Amount £	Debit ✓	Credit ✓
Gringles Co	300	✓	
Lester plc	1,308	✓	
Shrier Goods	2,676	✓	
Abunda Bags	1,992	✓	

(b)

General ledger

Account name	Amount £	Debit ✓	Credit ✓
Sales ledger control	6,276	✓	
Sales	5,230		✓
VAT	1,046		✓

Task 1.2

(a)

Purchases ledger

Account name	Amount £	Debit ✓	Credit ✓
Frankie's Leatherware	12,348		✓
Casaubon's	3,924		✓

(b)

General ledger

Account name	Amount £	Debit ✓	Credit ✓
Purchases ledger control	16,272		✓
Purchases	13,560	✓	
VAT	2,712	✓	

Task 1.3

(a)

Purchases ledger

Account name	Amount £	Debit ✓	Credit ✓
Casaubon's	2,445	✓	

(b)

General ledger

Account name	Amount £	Debit ✓	Credit ✓
Purchases ledger control	2,445	✓	
Purchases	510	✓	
VAT	102	✓	

(c)

General ledger

Account name	Amount £	Debit ✓	Credit ✓
Sales ledger control	3,984		✓
Sales ledger control	56		✓
Discounts allowed	56	✓	

Task 1.4

(a)

General ledger

Account name	Amount £	Debit ✓	Credit ✓
VAT	7.04	✓	
Office expenses	37.80	✓	
Travel	27.00	✓	
Purchases	20.00	✓	

(b) The correct answer is: £91.84

Working

(7.04 + 37.80 + 27.00 + 20.00)

Task 1.5

Purchases

Date 20XX	Details	Amount £	Date 20XX	Details	Amount £
01 Nov	Balance b/d	140,389			
15 Nov	Purchases ledger control	14,388			
30 Nov	Purchases ledger control	52,389			
			30 Nov	Balance c/d	207,166
	Total	207,166		Total	207,166
1 Dec	Balance b/d	207,166			

Bank interest received

Date 20XX	Details	Amount £	Date 20XX	Details	Amount £
			01 Nov	Balance b/d	32
			15 Nov	Bank	14
			30 Nov	Bank	22
30 Nov	Balance c/d	68			
	Total	68		Total	68
			1 Dec	Balance b/d	68

Task 1.6

Account name	Amount £	Debit £	Credit £
Maintenance expenses	6,082	6,082	
Cash at bank	22,241	22,241	
Capital	24,000		24,000
Heat and light	7,893	7,893	
Discounts allowed	2,409	2,409	
Discounts received	7,056		7,056
Motor expenses	7,435	7,435	
Machinery	36,000	36,000	
Computer equipment	8,018	8,018	
Sundry expenses	14,167	14,167	
Legal expenses	1,195	1,195	
Office expenses	1,221	1,221	
Petty cash	200	200	
Purchases	214,229	214,229	
Purchases ledger control	17,851		17,851
Rent and rates	6,976	6,976	
Sales	421,956		421,956
Sales ledger control	28,540	28,540	
Sales returns	7,252	7,252	
Inventory	38,414	38,414	
Bank interest received	1,253		1,253
Travel	1,096	1,096	
VAT owing to HM Revenue & Customs	15,892		15,892
Salaries	84,640	84,640	
Totals		488,008	488,008

Section 2

Task 2.1

Sales returns day book

Date 20XX	Details	Credit note number	Total £	VAT @ 20% £	Net £	Bags returns £	Suitcases returns £
30 Nov	Shrier Goods	562	624	104	520	520	
30 Nov	Gringles Co	563	408	68	340		340
30 Nov	Lester plc	564	1,068	178	890	890	
	Totals		2,100	350	1,750	1,410	340

Task 2.2

VAT: (15 × 23) × 0.85 × 0.2 = 58.65

Total: (15 × 23 × 0.85) + 58.65 = 351.90

	Yes ✓	No ✓
Has the correct purchase price of the cabin cases been charged?		✓
Has the correct discount been applied?		✓
What would be the VAT amount charged if the invoice was correct?	£	58.65
What would be the total amount charged if the invoice was correct?	£	351.90

Task 2.3

(a)

Supplier code	PL244
General ledger code	GL001

(b) The correct answer is: product code

....

Task 2.4

(a) The correct answer is: discount of £10

(b) The correct answer is: credit note C579

(c) The correct answer is: £6,141

Working

(6,151 – 10)

....

Task 2.5

(a)

Sumberton Ltd
Sumberton House
10 Main Road
Sawlow
SA7 5LD

REMITTANCE ADVICE

To: Frankie's Leatherware   Date: 31 December 20XX

Please find attached our cheque in payment of the following amounts.

Invoice number	Credit note number	Amount £
29333		3,222
	176	337
Total amount paid		2,885

(b) The correct answer is: an invoice adds to the amount owed to the supplier

....

Task 2.6

(a)

Sumberton Ltd
Sumberton House,
10 Main Road
Sawlow
SA7 5LD

VAT Registration No. 536 3723 77

Gringles Co   Customer account code: SL637
Unit 18 Radley Estate
Sawlow
SA7 7VB

Date: 22 December 20XX

Invoice No:12901
Delivery note number: 6734527

Quantity of goods	Product code	Total list price £	Net amount after bulk discount £	VAT £	Gross £
80	L736B	1,600.00	1,360.00	261.12	1,621.12

(b) The correct answer is: trade discount

....

Task 2.7

Sumberton Ltd
Sumberton House
10 Main Road
Sawlow
SA7 5LD

To: Diamond Bags   Date: 31 December 20XX

Date 20XX	Details	Transaction amount £	Outstanding amount £
10 December	Invoice 12905	1,902	1,902
12 December	Credit note 701	219	1,683
30 December	Invoice 12916	733	2,416
31 December	Cheque	1,668	748
31 December	Discount taken	15	733

Task 2.8

(a) The correct answer is: sales invoice 12813
(b) The correct answer is: £2,304 ((2,000 × 96/100) + 384)
(c) The correct answer is: £2,384 (2,000 + 384)

Task 2.9

Item	Capital expenditure ✓	Revenue expenditure ✓	Capital income ✓	Revenue income ✓
Payment in advance for 3 months of phone line rental		✓		
Proceeds from sale of machinery			✓	
Sale of suitcases for cash				✓
Receipt of payment from trade receivable for bags				✓
Purchase of a shop building	✓			
Petty cash payment for stationery		✓		

Task 2.10

(a)

	True ✓	False ✓
The book of original entry for discounts allowed is the petty cash book		✓
Input tax is the VAT suffered on purchases	✓	
A goods received note is a primary document for recording in the accounting records		✓

(b)

Item	Example
Asset	Trade receivables
Liability	Bank overdraft
Capital transaction	Drawings

Notes

Notes